50

American Serial Killers You've Probably Never Heard Of

Volume Two

Robert Keller

**Please Leave Your Review of This Book At
http://bit.ly/kellerbooks**

ISBN-13: 978-1535138376

ISBN-10: 1535138378

© 2016 by Robert Keller

robertkellerauthor.com

All rights reserved.

No part of this publication may be copied or reproduced in any format, electronic or otherwise, without the prior, written consent of the copyright holder and publisher. This book is for informational and entertainment purposes only and the author and publisher will not be held responsible for the misuse of information contain herein, whether deliberate or incidental.

Much research, from a variety of sources, has gone into the compilation of this material. To the best knowledge of the author and publisher, the material contained herein is factually correct. Neither the publisher, nor author will be held responsible for any inaccuracies.

Table of Contents

Richard Angelo 7
Richard Biegenwald 10
Terry Blair 14
Shelly Andre Brooks 18
Ricardo Caputo 22
James and Susan Carson 26
Jarvis Catoe 30
Thor Nis Christiansen 33
Tony Costa 36
Thomas Dillon 40
Ronald Dominique 44
Mack Ray Edwards 47
Walter Ellis 50
Scott Thomas Erskine 53
Richard Evonitz 57
John Fautenberry 61
Sean Vincent Gillis 64
Sean Patrick Goble 68
Mark Goudeau 72
Vaughn Greenwood 75
William Hance 79

Michael Hughes 83

Leslie Irvin 86

Philip Carl Jablonski 90

Calvin Jackson 93

Milton Johnson 97

Vincent Johnson 100

Roger Kibbe 104

Tillie Klimek 108

Timothy Krajcir 111

Peter Kudzinowski 115

DeVernon LeGrand 117

Michael Lee Lockhart 121

Orville Lynn Majors 124

Richard Marquette 127

Rhonda Bell Martin 130

Winston Moseley 133

Louise Peete 136

Steven Pennell 140

Thomas Piper 143

Paul Dennis Reid Jr. 146

Robert Shulman 149

Robert Silveria Jr. 153

Morris Solomon Jr. 156

Timothy Spencer 159

Paul Michael Stephani 163

Maury Travis 166

50 American Monsters You've Probably Never Heard Of Volume 2

Nathaniel White 169
Scott Williams 172
Martha Woods 175

Richard Angelo

Richard Angelo never wanted to hurt anyone. All he wanted to do was create a situation where he could show his expertise and come out looking like a hero. After all, he'd being doing that all his life. The former Eagle Scout and volunteer fireman was admired by friends and neighbors alike for his devotion to duty. It instilled in him an obsessive need for recognition – an obsession that would have tragic results for the patients of Good Samaritan Hospital, in West Islip, New York.

After graduating from New York State University in May 1985, Angelo worked as a registered nurse at two Long Island hospitals. In April 1987, he found employment at Good Samaritan Hospital where he was assigned to the night shift, on a ward for intensive care patients. Angelo was quite happy to work the 11 p.m. to 7 a.m. stretch. In fact, he seemed to prefer it.

In the latter months of 1987, staff doctors at Good Samaritan started picking up some unusual patterns. Patients who appeared to be recovering from surgery were suddenly deteriorating and dying for no apparent reason. Hospital administrators were both perplexed and alarmed. Especially when the rate accelerated and there were six suspicious deaths in under a month between September and October.

Then, on October 11, an incident occurred that blew the case wide open. Patient Girolamo Cucich was approached by a bearded man in a hospital uniform who informed him, "I'm going to make you feel better," before injecting something into his I.V. tube. Almost immediately, Cucich experienced numbness and felt his chest constrict. Drawing on his last ounce of strength, the patient pressed the buzzer to summon a nurse. The action saved his life, and no doubt those of countless other patients as well.

On October 12, police questioned Richard Angelo, the only bearded nurse on the hospital's staff, about the incident. Angelo denied any contact with the patient, but after lab tests found traces of Pavulon (a drug that produces muscular paralysis) in Cucich's blood, the police obtained a warrant for Angelo's locker. Inside, they found hypodermic needles and a vial of potassium chloride, a drug that can induce cardiac arrest if misused. Angelo had no need for this drug, neither was he authorized to have it in his possession.

On November 14, detectives searched Angelo's apartment and took into evidence vials of Pavulon and Anectine (a similar drug). Angelo was arrested the following day, while attending an out-of-town conference for emergency medical technicians.

In custody, he confessed to a series of murders, admitting that he injected on average two patients per week with Pavulon or Anectine. Asked why he'd done it, Angelo told investigators: "I wanted to create a situation where I would cause the patient to have some respiratory distress or some problem, and through my intervention or suggested intervention or whatever, come out looking like I knew what I was doing. I had no confidence in myself. I felt very inadequate."

The only problem with this plan was that, more often than not, Angelo was not able to save the patient. In his last six weeks on the job, there were 37 "Code Blue" emergencies, during which 25 patients died. A conservative estimate put the number of Angelo's victims at 38.

Angelo would eventually be convicted of two counts of second-degree murder, one count of second-degree manslaughter, one count of criminally negligent homicide, and six counts of assault. He was sentenced to a term of 61 years to life.

Richard Biegenwald

Richard Biegenwald had a troubled start to life. The son of an abusive alcoholic, he suffered regular beatings as a child. In retaliation, he burned down the family home and was sent for psychiatric observation. He was just 5-years-old at the time.

By age eight, Richard was a habitual drinker and gambler; at 11, he received a series of electroshock therapy treatments at New York's Bellevue Hospital. A year later, he lit himself on fire in an apparent suicide attempt. Sent to the State Training School for Boys in Warwick, New York, he was soon in trouble again, for theft and for inciting other inmates to escape.

With a background like that, it was always likely that Biegenwald would turn to a life of crime, and so it proved. Arrested at 16 for transporting a stolen car across state lines, he spent a few months in a juvenile correctional facility. It did little to discourage him. Shortly after his release, he and another youth stole a car and held up a liquor store. In the process, Biegenwald shot and killed the proprietor, Stephen Sladowski, a 47-year-old father of four.

Biegenwald and his partner were arrested in Maryland two days later, after Biegenwald fired a shotgun at state troopers who had pulled them over for speeding. Convicted of murder, he was sentenced to life imprisonment. He was released on parole in 1975, having served just 17 years.

Back on the streets, Biegenwald worked a number of odd jobs, but he soon fell foul of the law, first for failing to report to his parole officer and then for a 1980 rape. The charge was eventually dropped, but he was returned to prison to serve six months for the parole violation.

Biegenwald had married in the interim and upon his release he and his wife moved to Asbury Park, New Jersey, where he found work as a maintenance man. Also living in his new apartment block was an ex-con, Dherran Fitzgerald. The two men struck up an acquaintanceship and began hanging out together.

On January 4, 1983, the body of 18-year-old Anna Olesiewicz was found behind a restaurant in Ocean Township, north of Asbury Park. She'd last been seen on the Asbury Park boardwalk on August 28, 1982. Anna had been shot four times in the head, but police were confused as to the motive. The corpse was fully clothed and there was no evidence of rape.

Upon hearing of the recovery of the body, a girlfriend of Biegenwald's wife placed a call to the police and accused

Biegenwald of the crime. Biegenwald was arrested on January 22, along with his cohort, Dherran Fitzgerald. A search of his apartment turned up pipe bombs, pistols, a machine gun, knockout drops and marijuana, a live puff adder, and the floor plans of various local businesses.

In custody, Fitzgerald quickly rolled on his partner and told police about two corpses buried at the home of Biegenwald's mother, on Staten Island.

Following Fitzgerald's directions, investigators dug up the remains of 17-year-old Maria Ciallella, last seen in October 1981, and Deborah Osborne, also 17, missing since April 1982. Ciallella had been shot twice in the head; Osborne had been stabbed in the chest and abdomen.

Fitzgerald later led officers to another grave, that of 17-year-old Betsy Bacon. She'd been shot twice in the head and buried to the north of Asbury Park. Another excavation yielded the body of William Ward, a drug dealer and prison escapee. Like the other victims, Ward had been killed by gunshot wounds to the head, five in his case. He was found buried outside of Neptune City, New Jersey. Biegenwald was also suspected, but never charged, in two other murders.

Biegenwald was indicted on five counts of first-degree murder, and with Dherran Fitzgerald testifying for the prosecution, the outcome was always a formality. He was found guilty and sentenced to die by lethal injection. The sentenced was later overturned by an Appellate Court and commuted to life in prison without the possibility of parole.

Richard Biegenwald died at St. Francis Medical Center in Trenton, New Jersey on March 10, 2008. Cause of death was given as respiratory and kidney failure. He was 67 years old.

Terry Blair

Given Terry Blair's family history, it was an even bet that he'd end up on the wrong side of the law. His brother, Walter Blair Jr., was executed for murder in 1993; half-brother, Clifford Miller, drew a 240-year term for attempted murder, kidnapping, rape and forced sodomy; mother, Janice Blair, shot a man to death but entered an Alford plea (effectively, no contest) and escaped jail time.

By the time he came under suspicion for a series of prostitute murders, Terry Blair himself had already spent 21 years behind bars for killing Angela Monroe, the pregnant mother of his two children. Angry with Monroe for continuing to work as a prostitute, Blair had beaten the woman to death.

That was in 1982 and Blair had served 21 years of a 25-year sentence before being released in 2003. Not long after, he was returned to prison for a parole violation, but by June, he was back on the streets. Unbeknownst to the authorities, Blair had already committed murder during his brief period of freedom, strangling prostitute Nellia Harris to death.

On June 14, the body of 42-year-old Kansas City prostitute, Anna Ewing, was found on a vacant lot. She'd been strangled with such force that her neck was broken.

Prostitute murders are notoriously difficult to solve and the police did not hold out much hope of an arrest unless the killer struck again. They were unprepared, though, for the unprecedented murder spree that Terry Blair would unleash.

Blair hated prostitutes, a point he'd make forcibly to acquaintances at every opportunity. He'd spent 21 years in prison stewing over this hatred. Now it erupted in an orgy of violence that claimed five more lives in the space of just two days. Patricia Wilson Butler, 58, died on September 2, 2004, the same night that 38-year-old Sheliah McKinzie was strangled to death. Two days later Blair outdid even that spree, killing three women on September 4. Darci Williams, 25, Carmen Hunt, 40, and 31-year-old Claudette Juniel were all strangled to death. Juniel, in addition, suffered a broken neck.

The bodies still lay undiscovered when an anonymous tipster placed a call to 911 on September 4 and told the dispatcher where one of the victims could be found.

"How do you know a dead body is there?" the dispatcher asked.

"I put it there," the caller answered, adding, "Look up under the branches, under the bushes by the alley. It's an abandoned house. It's red."

The dispatcher then asked for the victim's name to which the caller responded.

"She's a prostitute, like the other two."

"You killed them also?" the dispatcher asked

"Yeah," the caller said, before hanging up.

A day later, the anonymous caller again rang 911. This time, he reported two more bodies, referring to them as scum. He promised to call again and said there were six bodies in all. Terry Blair would be arrested before he had time to make that call.

On October 15, 2004, Blair was charged with six counts of first-degree murder, one count of first-degree assault, and three counts of forcible rape.

In exchange for the prosecution dropping two additional charges against him (for the murders of prostitutes Sandra Reed and Nellia Harris) and for not seeking the death penalty, Blair agreeing to waive his right to a jury trial. Kansas City prosecutors had offered a similar deal to serial killer Lorenzo Gilyard a year earlier.

Blair was ultimately found guilty and sentenced to life in prison without the possibility of parole. He is currently incarcerated at the Potosi Correctional Center in Mineral Point, Missouri.

Shelly Andre Brooks

The stereotypical public perception of a sexual psychopath is of a hyper-intelligent charmer capable of lulling his victims into a false sense of security before striking. That description might hold true for the likes of Ted Bundy or Christopher Wilder. Shelly Andre Brooks, though, is about as far removed from suave as you could hope to get.

Abandoned by his mother while still in his teens, Brooks was raised by his maternal grandmother until he dropped out of school in the 11th grade. He then drifted into a life of menial jobs and petty crime, before eventually becoming homeless at the age of 27. He'd spend the next ten years living on the streets, in abandoned buildings, and in his brother-in-law's basement. During that time he committed seven murders (and possibly as many as 14).

His first known victim was 53-year-old Sandra Davies, bludgeoned to death in the Garland neighborhood of Detroit on August 31, 2001. According to Brooks' they went to an abandoned building to have sex, but got into an altercation after he demanded his money back. When Davies tried to leave, he struck her repeatedly on the head with a brick, then dragged her into a closet and left her to die. Davies's decomposed corpse was found on August 31, 2001.

On January 22, 2002, Pamela Greer, 33, was found in the same building, her body partially consumed by animals. Three months later the battered corpse of Marion Woods-Daniels, 36, was found in a house on nearby Crane Street. Brooks claimed he'd killed her after she tried to cheat him out of money he'd paid her for sex.

Rhonda Myles, 45, was found in a vacant building on April 22, 2002. She'd been beaten to death with the leg of a wooden chair. Brooks' DNA would later be found on the murder weapon.

On November 5, 2002, a pedestrian walking near the corner of Mack and Holcomb Streets, found the body of 30-year-old Thelma Johnson. She had been bludgeoned about the head and face with a blunt object.

The next to die was 38-year-old Melissa Toston. Her body was discovered on October 18, 2005. It was estimated that she'd been dead four days. Brooks later testified that he beat Tolson to death with a concrete block found at the scene, cutting himself in the process. Blood found near the victim was matched to Brooks.

On June 5, the body of an unidentified victim was found at 2646 Harding. The M.O. did not match that of the earlier victims but Brooks later confessed to throttling the woman to death, allegedly in a dispute over money.

By now, police had a trail of dead bodies found naked and spread-eagled in abandoned buildings. However, they had no leads on the killings and although Shelly Brooks was more or less a fixture in the area, he was not considered a suspect. All who knew him regarded the polite, mild-mannered Brooks as harmless.

On June 26, 2006, Brooks lured another prostitute to an abandoned building, although this victim would survive his deadly attentions. According to the woman's later testimony, she and Brooks smoked crack cocaine inside a garage, then went to an abandoned house where Brooks sexually assaulted her and then struck her repeatedly on the head with a brick and left her for dead.

Miraculously, the woman survived the attack although she was comatose for a number of weeks. When she regained consciousness she named her attacker as a man she knew only as "E." This was one of the street names used by Brooks and he was arrested soon after. Confronted with the evidence against him, Brooks confessed, even adding two murders that the police did not know about.

Brooks was charged with seven counts of first-degree murder dating from 1999 to 2005. On March 22, 2007, it took a jury just 30 minutes to find him guilty. On March 27, he drew a mandatory sentence of life in prison without the possibility of parole.

Ricardo Caputo

Richard Caputo was born in 1949 in Mendoza, Argentina, arriving in the United States on a six-month visa in 1970. He settled in New York City where he worked as a busboy at various restaurants and later became a barman at the Plaza Hotel. It was during this time that he met Natalie Brown, a 19-year-old teller at the bank where he cashed his paychecks. The handsome, smooth-talking Caputo soon talked Natalie into a date and before long they were an item.

Natalie's parents were against the relationship, but she was clearly taken with the young man. In the summer of 1971, she and Caputo went to Europe together and on their return they announced their engagement. But soon after, cracks began to appear in the relationship. More specifically, Natalie wanted out, Richard didn't want her to leave.

On the night of July 31, Natalie's parents went out to dinner, leaving her and Caputo at their home in Roslyn, Long Island. At around 8:30 p.m., Caputo called the police and told the dispatcher, "I think I killed my girlfriend." A unit immediately rushed to the house where they found Natalie Brown in the kitchen, stabbed to death.

Taken into custody, Caputo confessed immediately, explaining that he'd stabbed his fiancée over her decision to end their relationship. He was charged with murder but, after being examined by psychiatrists, was declared insane and unfit to stand trial.

Caputo was sent to Matteawan State Hospital, where he began receiving treatment from staff psychologist, Judith Becker. In October 1973, he was transferred to the Manhattan Psychiatric Center. Caputo was a model patient who was given free access to the hospital grounds and allowed to go out on furlough several times a week. On many of these occasions, he visited Judith Becker. There were suggestions of a romantic involvement, although Ms. Becker's parents vehemently deny this.

In October 1974, Judith asked Caputo to stop calling at her apartment, something that apparently angered him greatly. On October 21, after failing to raise Judith on the phone, her parents called at her home. They found her battered and strangled to death. Her 1972 Plymouth Duster was missing. So too, was Richard Caputo.

Caputo next showed up in San Francisco, where he assumed the alias Ricardo Dunoquir and wooed Barbara Ann Taylor, a 28-year-old manager at a company that made educational films. Caputo persuaded Taylor to let him move into her apartment. However, she soon tired of the arrangement when it became clear that he was sponging off her.

She asked him to leave, even buying him a plane ticket to Honolulu, where he planned to look for restaurant work. However, within two weeks, he was back. On March 27, Caputo was seen leaving Barbara Taylor's apartment with a suitcase. Three days later, Barbara failed to show up for dinner at her parents' home. Concerned, her parents called on her apartment. They found her beaten to death.

Caputo, meanwhile, had fled to Mexico City, where he adopted the name Ricardo Martinez Diaz, and found work in a bookstore. He also began dating a 20-year-old college student, named Laura Gomez. On October 3, 1977, Gomez was found bludgeoned to death in her apartment. Caputo was suspected but was nowhere to be found.

Caputo returned to the United States where he settled in the Southwest, married, and fathered two children. Seven years later, he deserted his family and fled to South America. Suspicions persist that Caputo's sudden departure had something to do with the death of New York writer, Jacqueline Bernard, 62, found strangled in her home on August 2, 1983. Caputo, however, denies any involvement in that crime.

Back in South America in 1984, Caputo added bigamy to his long list of crimes. He had two more children with his new wife before moving the family to the United States in 1985. They stayed several years, returning to South America soon after Caputo's case was featured on America's Most Wanted.

Caputo might have evaded the police indefinitely, but apparently, he could not evade his own conscience. According to his lawyer, Caputo began having nightmares about the killings and also felt his murderous urges returning. Fearing that he might kill again, he decided to give himself up.

On January 18, 1994, he appeared at a Manhattan police station and surrendered to authorities. In 1995, a New York court sentenced him to 25 years in prison. He died there in October 1997, at the age of 48.

James and Susan Carson

Mission based serial killers, those who believe they are acting on behalf of some higher power, most commonly target prostitutes. James Clifford Carson (aka Michael Bear Carson) and Susan Barnes Carson (aka Suzan Carson) targeted people they believed to be "witches," claiming three, and possibly as many as 12, victims.

And yet, this deadly duo makes the most unlikely of serial killer couples. Up until 1980, James Carson, a man with a master's degree in Chinese studies, was married and living in Phoenix, Arizona, with his wife and 4-year-old child. Susan Barnes was a recently divorced mother of two teenaged sons in nearby Scottsdale.

At around this time, James Carson's wife left him and fled to California with their daughter, citing his irrational behavior. James remained in Phoenix. Not long after, he met Susan Barnes and the two became involved in a relationship. Before long, they'd married, even though James was still legally married to his first wife. They moved to Garberville, California where they found work on a marijuana farm.

During this time they began experimenting with hallucinogenic drugs, and after one of their trips, Susan declared that she'd had a vision that they should adopt the Muslim faith and change their names to Suzan & Michael Bear. James readily agreed and although there is no evidence that they officially converted to Islam, they insisted on being called by their new names, became vegetarians, and began practicing yoga. They also became convinced that their friends and acquaintances were witches bent on the destruction of the world.

In early 1981, the couple moved to San Francisco. They committed their first murder in Haight-Ashbury in March of that year. The victim was their 22-year-old roommate, Keryn Barnes, who was bludgeoned with a frying pan before being stabbed 13 times. Thereafter, the Carsons wrapped her body in a blanket and hid it in the basement before fleeing.

Over the next two years, they remained at large, wandering the American Southwest and even (according to their later confession) traveling to Europe. They survived by selling drugs and became more and more involved in their delusions. They also committed at least two more murders.

Clark Stephens was killed near Alderpoint in Humboldt County, California, in 1982. He was shot, and his body burnt before being buried under a mound of chicken fertilizer. Carson later claimed they'd killed Stephens, who had worked with them on the marijuana farm, because he'd sexually assaulted Suzan.

Jon Charles Hillyar, 30, was murdered in January 1983, outside Santa Rosa, California. According to Carson, they met Hillyer while he was hitchhiking and killed him on the side of a road in Sonoma County, California, after he called Suzan a witch.

After their arrest in 1983, the Carsons called a press conference at which they confessed to the murders. During this interview, James Carson explained why the couple had murdered Keryn Barnes, claiming she'd falsely converted to Islam and had then begun draining Suzan of her "health and yogic powers."

James and Susan Carson went on trial in June 1984. Despite their earlier confession, they entered not guilty pleas to the murder of Keryn Barnes. On June 12, 1984, they were found guilty and sentenced to 25 years in prison. Convictions in the Stephens and Hillyar murders added a further 50 years to each of their sentences.

James Carson is currently serving his time at Mule Creek State Prison. Suzan Carson is incarcerated at Central California Women's Facility.

They are suspects in nearly a dozen other murders in the U.S. and Europe.

50 American Monsters You've Probably Never Heard Of Volume 2

Jarvis Catoe

On the morning of August 4, 1941, Evelyn Anderson, a 26-year-old waitress, left her home in the Bronx to walk to the restaurant where she worked. Evelyn never arrived for her shift that day. Her body was discovered in an alley at 9 o'clock that evening, strangled to death. Such was the violence of the attack that marks of the killer's fingernails were imprinted on her throat. Evelyn had not been sexually abused and the police, therefore, assumed that the motive had been robbery. Certainly, the victim's watch had been taken.

The watch showed up a few days later in a New York pawnshop, hocked by a man named Charles Woolfolk. Following up on this lead, detectives tracked down Woolfolk, who insisted that the watch had been given to him by a girlfriend, Hazel Johnson. According to Johnson, she'd gotten the watch from Mandy Reid and according to Reid, the watch, as well as a handbag, was a gift from a male acquaintance, Jarvis Catoe. Catoe lived in Washington D.C., she said, but he'd recently been in New York.

A call from the NYPD to their D.C. colleagues led to 36-year-old Catoe being hauled in for questioning. He quickly confessed to killing Anderson. But that wasn't all, he said. He'd also killed seven women in Washington and had committed four rapes, leaving his victims alive.

Catoe killed his first victim in 1935, raping and strangling Florence Darcy, a murder for which another man had been convicted and had already served five years in prison. Josephine Robinson was next, killed on December 1, 1939. Less than a year later, Catoe struck again, strangling two victims within months of each other - Lucy Kidwell in September 1940 and Mattie Steward in November that same year. The next victim was Ada Puller, killed on January 2, 1941.

Thus far, the murders had attracted little attention. The victims, like Catoe, were black, and the crimes had warranted only cursory police attention and even less interest from the media.

But all of that was to change on March 8, when newly married Rose Abramovitz saw Catoe loitering outside her house and offered him a job waxing her floor. Instead, he raped and strangled her before fleeing the scene with $20 taken from her purse.

The next murder caused an even bigger stir. During a Washington downpour on

June 15, Jesse Strieff, a pretty twenty-something secretary at the War Department, mistakenly got into Catoe's car, thinking it was a taxicab. Her nude body was found in a garage the following day. She'd been raped and strangled, her clothes removed from the scene.

The murder provoked a furious reaction on The Hill, spawning congressional investigations and a major shake-up of the Washington police department. Still, despite an intensive investigation, the case remained unsolved until Catoe eventually confessed.

Catoe was brought to trial in October 1941, charged with the murder of Rose Abramovitz. He sought to recant his confessions, claiming that the police had beaten them out of him. However, that was never going to cut much ice with the all-male, all-white jury, who took just 18 minutes to convict.

As a black man who'd murdered three white women, there was only ever going to be one outcome. Jarvis Catoe went to the electric chair in the District of Columbia on January 15, 1943.

Thor Nis Christiansen

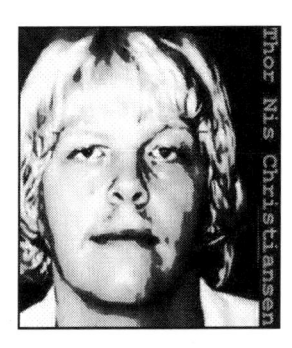

During late 1976 and early 1977, a serial killer terrorized female students on the campus of the University of California at Santa Barbara. The killer struck without warning, claiming three victims in a series of shootings that became known as the "Look-alike Murders," because the victims closely resembled one another.

The first victim was 21-year-old Jacqueline Rook, abducted from a bus stop in Goleta, Santa Barbara, on December 6, 1976. That same day, a Goleta waitress named Mary Sarris mysteriously disappeared. Both girls were still missing on January 18, when 21-year-old Patricia Laney, vanished without a trace.

Laney's corpse was discovered the next day, on an isolated road in the Santa Ynez Mountains, a bullet wound to the head from a small caliber pistol. Then, when Jacqueline Rook's decomposing remains were found on January 20, the authorities' worst fears were realized. Rook had a similar wound and was found in the same area. It appeared the Santa Barbara police were hunting a serial killer.

The discovery of the corpses led to widespread student protests and placed immense pressure on the police to solve the murders. They responded by questioning hundreds of people in connection with the crimes.

One of those was an overweight gas station attendant named Thor Nis Christiansen. Brought in originally as a minor found in possession of alcohol, Christiansen was questioned about the murders when a .22-caliber pistol was found in his car. However, he was not considered a serious suspect and was soon released. By the time the skeletal remains of Mary Sarris were discovered on May 22, Christiansen had decamped to Oregon and the murders had stopped.

Two years later, Christiansen had undergone a transformation, having lost weight, completed his high school diploma and moved back to Santa Barbara. He had not, however, lost his murderous compulsion.

On April 18, 1979, Linda Preston, 24, was thumbing rides in Hollywood, when Christiansen picked her up. They drove several blocks before he suddenly drew a pistol and fired at her, hitting her in the left ear. Despite being seriously injured Preston managed to throw herself from the car and escape on foot.

Three months later, on July 11, Preston was at the Bottom Line Bar in Hollywood when she spotted her assailant. She immediately called the police who arrived soon after to take Christiansen into custody. He was charged with felonious assault.

Then Santa Barbara police picked up on the arrest and noted similarities between the attack on Linda Preston and the Look-alike murders. They also noted that Christiansen had been living in Santa Barbara at the time and had been arrested while in possession of a .22-caliber pistol.

Christiansen was questioned in connection with the killings on July 27. Soon after, he was formally charged with three counts of first-degree murder in Santa Barbara. A fourth charge was added in Los Angeles, relating to the May 26 discovery of murder victim, Laura Sue Benjamin.

Christiansen went on trial in early 1980. He initially entered a plea of "not guilty by reason of insanity," but he later changed his plea to guilty. The motive for the murders, he said, was an obsessive need to have sex with corpses.

As there was no death penalty in California at the time, Christiansen was sentenced to life in prison. He was stabbed to death at Folsom State Prison on March 30, 1981. The assailant has never been identified.

Tony Costa

Tony Costa was tried and found guilty of murdering and dismembering four young women in Cape Cod between 1966 and 1969. That much is known. What is not known is the full extent of his crimes, including perhaps as many as eight victims. What is not known is his motive, speculated to include necrophilia and cannibalism.

The first victims linked to Costa were a couple of hippy girls named Bonnie Williams and Diane Federoff. In June 1966, Costa informed his wife of three years that he was leaving, driving Williams and Federoff to Pennsylvania and then heading out to California by himself. Ten days later, he was back home in Massachusetts, telling his wife he'd driven the girls all the way to Hayward California. He told a similar story to the police when they came asking. Williams and Federoff were never seen or heard from again.

Costa did eventually go to California in January 1968, deserting his wife and three children in the process. He made his way to San Francisco's swinging Haight-Ashbury district, where he shacked up with Barbara Spaulding. In May of that year, Spaulding left her young son with relatives, saying she was going to Massachusetts with Costa. She was never seen again.

Back home in Massachusetts, Costa broke into a doctor's office on May 17, netting drugs and surgical instruments worth an estimated $5,000. A week later, 18-year-old Sydney Monzon vanished from her home in Provincetown. It would be 10 months before the truth about her disappearance was known.

By August, Costa's wife had divorced him, and by September 10, he had a new live-in lover, Susan Perry. A week later, Susan was gone. Costa told friends that she'd left him and gone to Mexico.

Costa was arrested for failing to pay child support in September and was held in custody until November 8. Shortly after his release, he started spending time with Christine Gallant. Like most women who associated with Tony Costa, Gallant was soon dead. She was found in her bathtub on November 23, having apparently drowned after a drug overdose.

On January 24, 1969, Patricia Walsh and Mary Anne Wysocki disappeared while on a visit to Provincetown. A massive search was launched and two weeks later turned up a dismembered female corpse near the Old Truro cemetery. It wasn't either of the missing girls, though, it was Susan Perry who'd gone missing in September having apparently left Costa to travel to Mexico.

The dismembered bodies of Walsh and Wysocki would eventually be found on March 4, along with Sydney Monzon, missing since May 1968. All three were interred in a shallow grave. Walsh and Wysocki had both been shot in the head, while all three bodies bore bite marks and signs of necrophilia.

In the course of their inquiries, investigators learned that Walsh and Wysocki had been seen in the company of Tony Costa shortly before their disappearance. When they went to question Costa, they found that he was in possession of the murdered girls' car. Costa claimed he'd bought the car from them and even produced a suspicious-looking bill of sale. According to him, Walsh and Wysocki had said they were going to Canada.

The detectives weren't buying it, and once they learned that the burial site was in a clearing that Costa used for growing marijuana, he was taken into custody. Under interrogation, Costa told several conflicting stories and although he readily agreed to a polygraph, it only served to convince investigators of his guilt.

Costa's trial began on May 6, 1970. It ended on May 29 with his conviction on four counts of murder. He was sentenced to life imprisonment, to be served at Walpole Prison.

Four years later, on Sunday, May 12, 1974, a guard doing a routine inspection found Costa hanging by the neck from a leather belt knotted around the upper bars of his cell. His death was ruled a suicide.

Thomas Dillon

Between April 1989 and April 1992, Ohio authorities were perplexed by a series of seemingly motiveless shootings. The sniper struck at random, taking down hunters, campers, and joggers with single shots from a high-powered rifle. By the time he was done, five men lay dead.

The first murder occurred near the small community of New Philadelphia, some 100 miles south of Cleveland. On April 1, 1989, Donald Welling, 35, was jogging along a quiet road when he passed a man sitting in a pickup. Welling had time to flash the stranger a smile and call a greeting before Thomas Dillon raised his rifle and fired, killing him instantly. Later Dillon would claim that a voice in his head had instructed him to open fire.

No shell casings were found at the murder site and with nothing to go on the case soon went cold. Nearly two years passed. Then the sniper was back with a vengeance. On November 10, 1990, Jamie Paxton was shot dead while hunting outside of St. Clairsville, Ohio. Just over two weeks later, Massachusetts native, Kevin Loring was shot and killed while on a hunting trip in Muskingum County.

After those two murders, the sniper went quiet again, re-emerging on March 14, 1992, to kill 49-year-old Claude Hawkins, as he fished in Coshocton County. The last to die was West Virginia resident Gary Bradley, shot while fishing in Noble County on April 5, 1992. The father of three was 44-years-old at the time of his death.

By this time, Ohio investigators had picked up a pattern. All of the shootings (except Loring) had occurred over a weekend and all were shot with a high-powered rifle, most likely fired from a vehicle parked on a nearby road. And yet no shell casings were found and no one had seen a car in the vicinity of the murders.

As the police fretted over whether they would ever solve the crimes, the killer himself threw them a clue. He wrote a letter to the local newspaper.

"I am the murderer of Jamie Paxton," he proclaimed. "Jamie Paxton was a complete stranger to me. I never saw him before in my life and he never said a word to me that Saturday. The motive for the murder was this - the murder itself."

The letter was promptly sent to the FBI's Behavioral Science Unit with a request for a profile. The report they produced described an educated white male who would have committed other crimes, like arson, and killing pets and farm animals. Although he might be a family man, he'd be a loner with a drinking problem. The murders would likely have been committed while he was under the influence of alcohol.

In these respects the profile was correct. However, the report also said that the killer would live near the crime scenes and would be in his twenties. Dillon was 42 when he was arrested and drove hundreds of miles to commit his crimes.

However, the profile did help investigators zero in on a suspect. Especially after a high school buddy of Dillon's came forward and raised suspicions about him. Richard Fry told investigators about Dillon's preoccupation with serial killers, his long drives through the backwoods of Ohio, and his boasts about setting more than 100 fires and killing more than 1,000 pets and farm animals.

Armed with this information Tuscarawas County detectives placed Dillon under surveillance. Over the next month, they watched him buying guns, taking long drives through the country and stopping to fire at street signs and animals, even driving to Massachusetts to visit Kevin Loring's grave.

Eventually, on November 27, 1992, FBI agents moved in to arrest Dillon on a federal weapons charge, relating to possession of a silencer. With their man in custody, the authorities held a press conference during which they asked anyone who'd done firearms transactions with Dillon to come forward.

On December 4, a gun dealer brought in a Mauser rifle that Dillon had sold him on April 6, the day after Gary Bradley was killed. Ballistics tests proved that it was the weapon that had killed both Bradley and Claude Hawkins.

Faced with the evidence against him, Dillon struck a deal, pleading guilty to five counts of murder in order to avoid the death penalty. He was sentenced to five consecutive life terms, to be served at Southern Ohio Correctional Facility in Lucasville.

Ronald Dominique

Houma, Louisiana, is a small, sleepy town in Terrebonne Parish in the southeastern part of the state. Nothing much happens here, although the town does have a close-knit gay community and a number of nightspots catering to them. For almost a decade, from 1997 to 2006, a member of that community, a pudgy, non-threatening man who walked with a limp, operated as a serial killer. His name was Ronald Dominique, and he is responsible for at least 23 murders.

Typical of most serial killers, Dominique had a predator's eye for the weak, the vulnerable, and the easily led. He targeted hustlers, drug addicts and the homeless, luring them back to his trailer on Blue Bayou Road with promises of cash for sex, or (if the victim was straight) with the prospect of sex with Dominique's fictitious wife. Once they reached the trailer, Dominique would ask the potential victim if he could tie him up. If the man refused, he was allowed to walk away unharmed. If however, he relented,

Dominique would bind and then rape him, before strangling him to death. The body would then be dumped in a sugarcane field, a ditch or a bayou in any of six southeast Louisiana parishes.

The first body – that of 19-year-old David Levron Mitchell – turned up near Hahnville in early 1997. Six months later, the strangled corpse of 20-year-old Gary Pierre was found in St. Charles Parish, and in July 1998, the body of 38-year-old Larry Ranson was discovered, also in St. Charles Parish.

The Ranson murder confirmed investigators' fears that a serial killer was at work in the area. Still, the killings of vagrants, addicts and hustlers did not raise much public ire and despite a lack of progress in the case, it was not until March 2005 that the Louisiana State Police, the FBI, and several parish Sheriff's departments came together to form a task force. By then, 23 men were dead.

When the case eventually resolved itself in November 2006, it was a tip from a parolee, rather than investigative effort, that cracked it. The ex-con told his parole officer about an encounter with a man named Ron, who he'd met in a bar. Ron, he said, had propositioned him to go back to his camper with the offer of having sex with his wife. Once they got there, however, Ron insisted on tying him up, claiming that his wife was "shy." The ex-con refused and Ron did not push the issue, allowing him to leave unharmed. However, the encounter had spooked him. He was certain that if he'd allowed himself to be tied up, he'd have been killed.

The parole officer passed the information on to the task force and although the ex-con did not know Ron's address he was able to lead investigators back to the trailer.

"Ron" turned out to be Ronald Dominique. Brought in for questioning in November 2006, Dominique voluntarily provided a DNA swab, which would link him to the murders of 19-year-old Manuel Reed and 27-year-old Oliver Lebanks.

Dominique had in the interim moved from his trailer to the Bunkhouse homeless shelter in Houma, and it was there that he was taken into custody on December 1, 2006. Soon after his arrest, he confessed to 23 murders. He would eventually be tried for eight.

On September 23, 2008, Ronald Dominique was sentenced to eight life terms after pleading guilty in order to avoid the death penalty. He is currently incarcerated at the Louisiana State Penitentiary in Angola.

Mack Ray Edwards

On March 5, 1970, a Caltrans employee named Mack Ray Edwards walked into a Los Angeles police station, placed a loaded handgun on the front desk, and told the stunned duty officer, "I have a guilt complex." He then went on to confess to the kidnapping of three young girls aged between 12 and 14, from their home in Sylmar, Los Angeles the previous day. Two of the girls had escaped but the third was still missing –until Edwards directed police to a location in Angeles National Forest, where she was found, unharmed.

Delighted that they'd found the missing girl alive, the authorities prepared to charge Edwards and a teenaged accomplice with kidnapping. Before they could do so, Edwards informed them that he had, "other matters to discuss." Then, as dumbstruck detectives listened, he confessed to six child murders, dating back to the early 1950s.

The first victim was Stella Nolan, eight years old at the time of her disappearance in June 1953. Stella had been snatched from her home in Compton and her fate had remained a mystery for sixteen long years. Now at least her family would have some closure.

Edwards waited three years before committing his next crime. This time, he abducted and killed two young victims, 13-year-old Don Baker and 11-year-old Brenda Howell. They went missing on August 6, 1956, and were never seen again.

According to Edwards, he'd been racked by guilt after the double homicide and had sworn off murder, managing to keep his inner demons at bay for 12 years. Then, on November 26, 1968, he'd struck again, shooting 16-year-old Gary Rochet to death near his home in Granada Hills. Three weeks later, he'd abducted and killed Roger Madison, also 16, in Sylmar. Finally, on May 16, 1969, he'd killed 13-year-old Donald Todd in Pacoima. Todd's body had not yet been found.

It was a lot to absorb and despite Edwards' obvious knowledge of the crimes, a number of investigators did not believe him. Their skepticism appeared to be vindicated on March 7, 1970, when Edwards led officers into the San Gabriel Mountains, in a search for the graves of victims Baker and Howell and came up empty. Four days later, though, Edwards led the police to a site beside the Santa Ana Freeway, where the skeletal remains of Stella Nolan were unearthed. As for the victims of his later killing spree, Edwards insisted that he'd buried them under sections of the L.A. freeway system, where he'd been working at the time as a heavy-equipment operator. The authorities declined to dig up the highway in order to find out if he was telling the truth. The murders, Mack said, had all been motivated by his overactive sex-drive.

The thing that bothered investigators most about Edwards' confession was his proclaimed 12-year hiatus. It is unusual for a serial killer to have such a long gap between murders and an inquiry into unsolved child murders committed during that period turned up 22 cases bearing an M.O. similar to that of Edwards. Yet the killer remained adamant that he'd killed no more than six.

He was equally adamant about what fate he deserved, telling the jury at his trial, "I want the chair. That's what I've always wanted."

The judge was happy to oblige him, sentencing Edwards to death for the six murders he'd committed. But that wasn't good enough for Edwards. He wanted to be executed immediately and after being told that he'd have to go through the mandatory appeals process first, he decided to take matters into his own hands. After two failed suicide attempts he eventually succeeded in hanging himself in his cell on October 30, 1971.

Walter Ellis

It was one of the most frustrating murder investigations the Milwaukee Police department had ever undertaken, the 21-year hunt for the serial slayer known as the "North Side Strangler." By the time it was resolved, a major overall to the state of Wisconsin's DNA gathering procedures would be called for, the failure of these having allowed the killer to remain at large long enough to commit one final atrocity.

The Strangler first came to police attention in 1986, when two strangled corpses were discovered in the space of as many days. Deborah Harris, 31, was fished out of a local river on October 10. A day later, 19-year-old Tanya Miller was found strangled near an abandoned house. Like Harris, she was a prostitute.

The police did what they could to solve the murders, but with little evidence to go on, and the advent of DNA technology still in the future, their prospects were slim at best. Soon the crimes had faded from memory and joined the cold case database. No one suspected that they might be the work of a serial killer.

Nearly a decade later, on April 24, 1995, workers doing repairs on an empty homestead discovered the strangled corpse of 28-year-old Florence McCormick. Two months later, the owner of a vacant residence got a shock when he arrived to do some remodeling work. On the floor of the bedroom lay the strangled corpse of a woman, later identified as Sheila Farrior, 37.

On August 30, another body turned up, that of 16-year-old Jessica Payne. Unlike the other victims, who were African American prostitutes, Payne was white, and a runaway from South Milwaukee. Her throat was slashed and she was not initially connected to the other crimes until DNA provided a link. (Doubt still persists as to whether she was a North Side Strangler victim.)

Following the murder of Jessica Payne, the North Side Strangler again went into hiatus, re-emerging on June 20, 1997, to strangle 41-year-old Joyce Mims. Like many of the other victims, Mims was found when builders arrived to renovate an old house.

Another long break occurred before the killer returned to claim his final victim on April 27, 2007. Ouithreaun Stokes, 28, was found by city inspectors who went to appraise a vacant building. She'd been strangled to death.

By now, police knew that a serial killer was responsible for at least six of the seven murders, having established a DNA link between the crimes. They were equally certain that the man they sought had a criminal record and had more than likely served time in prison. How else could you explain the long breaks between the murders? Yet their search for a match on the state's recently established DNA database came up frustratingly empty.

It was only after an informant pointed a finger at an ex-con named Walter E. Ellis that the case began to move forward in earnest. Ellis had served four years of a five-year stretch for reckless endangerment and had a long rap sheet beside. His DNA should have been on record, yet somehow it wasn't.

Still, investigators managed to secure a search warrant for his apartment, and a sample taken from a toothbrush yielded a DNA match to the six victims. The police finally had their man and soon after it emerged why they hadn't caught him sooner. Ellis had persuaded another ex-con to provide a DNA sample in his stead.

Ellis pleaded "no contest" at his February 2011 trial. He was sentenced to seven life terms without the possibility of parole.

Scott Thomas Erskine

A commonality found in the personal history of many serial killers is childhood head trauma. This is certainly the case with Scott Thomas Erskine, a seemingly normal 5-year-old until he was struck by a car on the Pacific Coast Highway, outside San Diego, in 1968. Erskine remained in a coma for 60 hours after the accident, but emerged without apparent physical damage, although he frequently complained of headaches, and blackouts. His family also noticed subtle changes in his behavior.

From the age of 10, Erskine began sexually molesting his 6-year-old sister, forcing her to perform oral sex on him. Soon he began abusing her friends, threatening to kill them if they told anybody. But someone did eventually tell, and Erskine found himself confined to a juvenile detention facility. He escaped at age 15, raping a 13-year-old girl at knifepoint and attacking a 27-year-old jogger while he was at large.

In 1980, now aged 17, Erskine beat a 14-year-old boy unconscious during an attempted rape. That earned him another spell in juvenile prison, during which he raped another inmate. At his trial, Erskine's mother pleaded for him to be spared from adult prison but the judge was unmoved, sentencing him to four years. He was paroled in 1984.

Upon his release, Erskine began dating a woman named Deborah. The couple moved to Florida in 1988, where they were married and had a son, Brandon. However, the marriage was short-lived due to Erskine's physical abuse, which included kicking his wife in the stomach while she was pregnant.

After the break-up, Erskine returned to California. In 1993, he abducted a woman from a bus stop, held her captive in his home, and raped and sodomized her over several days before letting her go. He threatened the woman with her life if she went to the police but she reported him anyway, leading to a conviction for rape and kidnapping.

Erskine was sentenced to 70 years in prison. As a convicted sex offender, he was required to submit his DNA to the CODIS database.

In March 2001, San Diego Cold Case investigators were looking into an unsolved double homicide dating back to 1993. Jonathan Sellers and Charlie Keever, aged 9 and 13 respectively, disappeared on March 27, 1993, while riding their bicycles along a dry riverbed in Palm City. A jogger found their bodies two days later. Jonathan was hanging by his neck from a tree branch. He was naked from the waist down, his legs and arms bound, and his mouth gagged. His genitals showed obvious signs of sexual assault.

Charlie lay on the ground nearby, also naked from the waist down, legs and arms bound, mouth gagged. He had a rope around his neck and his genitals were bleeding from extensive bite marks. In addition, he'd been burned with a cigarette. The pathologist determined that he was alive when the bites and burns were inflicted.

A semen sample taken from Charlie's mouth and two cigarette butts found near the bodies both produced a DNA profile and when investigators entered it into CODIS, they got a hit. The DNA belonged to Scott Erskine.

Erskine went on trial in September 2003 and was found guilty. However, as the jury could not reach a unanimous decision on the sentence, the judge declared a mistrial on the penalty phase. In April 2004 Erskine went before a second jury to decide his fate. This time, the jury unanimously recommended the death penalty.

On September 1, 2004, a California judge upheld the jury's recommendation and sentenced Erskine to death. He was transported to San Quentin to await execution.

While in prison, Erskine's DNA was matched to an unsolved homicide in Florida. Renee Baker, 26, was murdered on June 23, 1989, in Palm Beach. Erskine, who lived in the area at the time, admitted to rape and murder and was sentenced to life in prison without parole. Investigators suspect that he may have been involved in several other unsolved homicides.

Richard Evonitz

Richard Marc Evonitz was born on July 29, 1963, in Columbia, South Carolina, the first of Joseph and Tess Evonitz's three children. His childhood was not a happy one, with his parents separating while he was a baby and again when he was about 12. Joseph was a heavy drinker and when he drank he belittled his family, with Richard bearing his share of abuse. Both parents also openly flaunted affairs before their eventual divorce in 1985.

Despite these upheavals, Evonitz did well in school, graduating from Irmo High School in 1980 at age 16. After school, he worked briefly as the manager of a Jiffy Lube outlet before joining the United States Navy. He served with distinction for eight years, earning a Good Conduct Medal and being honorably discharged in 1989.

Shortly before leaving the Navy, Evonitz married Bonnie Lou Gower, a 17-year-old friend of his sister, who he'd known since she was in the 6th grade. Meanwhile, he set up a business that sold compressors and grinding equipment. In 1996, his wife filed for divorce, saying that she'd met someone else and was moving to California. Devastated by the divorce, Evonitz talked of suicide, but instead directed his anger outwards, committing his first known murder in September 1996.

On September 9, 1996, Sofia Silva was doing her homework on the front steps of her family's home in Spotsylvania County, Virginia, when she disappeared. A massive search was launched, eventually turning up her body in a marsh six weeks later. She was found 20 miles from her home, wrapped in a white coverlet. Her pubic hair had been shaved and it was apparent that she'd been held somewhere other than the dumpsite, prior to her death.

Nine months after the murder of Sofia Silva, sisters Kristin and Kati Lisk, 15 and 12 years old respectively, disappeared shortly after arriving home from school in Fredericksburg, Virginia. Their father came home from work to find no trace of his daughters other than Kristin's school bag, lying in the front yard. The sisters were found dead five days later, their bodies dumped in a river 40 miles from their home. Like Silva, their pubic areas had been shaved and there was evidence that they'd been held captive. Water found in their lungs was not from the river.

It was obvious to the police that the man who'd murdered Sofia Silva was also the killer of the Lisk siblings and this was confirmed when DNA recovered from the victims matched. However, that knowledge brought them no closer to catching the killer and as the years slipped by, it seemed that he had gotten away with murder.

Richard Evonitz, meanwhile, was putting his life back together. After filing for bankruptcy in 1997, he'd had his house foreclosed in 1999, and had suffered another business failure. However, he'd remarried in 1999, and had moved with his new wife to South Carolina, where he found work as a salesman for an air-compressor company.

If Evonitz had managed to keep his head down, he would probably never have been caught. But that was never likely to happen. On June 24, 2002, the monster re-emerged, kidnapped a 15-year-old girl in Columbia, South Carolina, and drove her to his apartment. There, he held her captive for eighteen hours, raping her again and again. Fortunately, Evonitz got sloppy in tying up his victim and when he dozed off, she managed to escape and alert the authorities.

By the time police arrived Evonitz had fled. Three days later, on June 27, 2002, he was tracked to Sarasota, Florida. Evonitz refused to surrender, eventually shooting himself in the head when a police dog was sent in to flush him from his hideout.

A subsequent search of Evonitz's home turned up a footlocker containing what investigators consider "trophies" from various homicides, including the Lisk and Silva murders. Evonitz is a suspect in numerous unsolved murders in Virginia, South Carolina, California, and Florida. One case to which he is strongly linked is the 1996 murder of Alicia Reynolds in Culpeper, Virginia. A hand-drawn map found in his locker showed directions to the site where Reynolds' body was found.

John Fautenberry

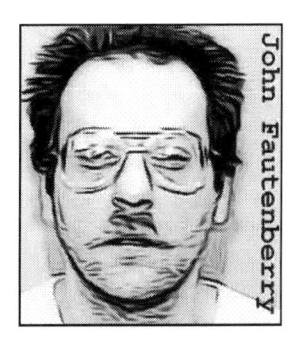

For some serial killers, the act of murder is a highly ritualized process involving planning, stalking, capturing and eventually the murder itself. For others, murder is a spur of the moment thing, carried out with no more thought than you or I would give to brushing our teeth. John Fautenberry falls into this latter class of killer.

What caused the former trucker and U.S. Navy man to go on his murderous 5-month campaign is unknown. What we do know is that, in October 1990, Fautenberry quit his job as a long-haul trucker and began thumbing rides along Oregon's freeways. In November of that year, he encountered Donald Nutley at a truck stop outside Portland. The two men struck up a conversation and before long, Nutley invited Fautenberry to go target shooting with him. Then Nutley made the critical mistake of telling Fautenberry that he was carrying $1,000 in cash. Fautenberry then promptly turned the gun on his new acquaintance, shot him in the head and relieved him of his money and vehicle.

In February 1991, Fautenberry was on route to Cincinnati, Ohio, when he met Gary Farmer, at another truck stop. Fautenberry pled poverty and Farmer offered to buy him breakfast and give him some money for gas. They went back to Farmer's truck where Fautenberry drew a gun and shot Farmer in the head, then took his wallet and left the scene.

After a brief stay with his sister in Cincinnati, Fautenberry hit the road again on February 17, 1991. Along a stretch of Interstate 275, he hitched a ride with Joseph Daron, who drove 10 miles out of his way to deliver Fautenberry to the intersection with Interstate 71. Fautenberry repaid Daron by shooting him twice in the chest. He then drove Daron's car south and dumped the man's body in a wooded area on the bank of the Ohio River, where it would be found more than a month later.

Fautenberry, meanwhile, had driven Daron's car to Portland, arriving there on February 24, 1991. Back in Oregon, he hooked up with some old friends along the coast. Through them, he met a woman named Christine Guthrie. The two began spending time together and when Fautenberry decided to go back to Portland, Guthrie went with him. Somewhere along the way, Fautenberry stopped on a quiet road, walked Guthrie into the woods and shot her three times in the back of the head. Taking Guthrie's bankcard, he cleaned out her account before hitting the road again.

March 13, 1991, found him in Juneau, Alaska, where he met Jefferson Diffee at a local bar. As Fautenberry didn't have a place to stay, Diffee's said he could crash at his apartment. As soon as they got there, Fautenberry overpowered his host, cuffed him, and then stabbed him to death. This time, though, Fautenberry had been careless. He'd been seen leaving the bar with his victim and he soon found himself under arrest. In Fautenberry's possession were several items taken from his earlier victims, including Joseph Daron's briefcase, wristwatch, and Bible.

On March 17, 1991, while in police custody, Fautenberry contacted FBI Agent Larry Ott and confessed to the murders of Nutley, Farmer, Daron, and Guthrie.

In August 1991, he pled guilty in an Alaskan state court to the murder of Jefferson Diffee and was sentenced to 99 years in prison. In September 1991, he was returned to Ohio, to stand trial for the murder of Joseph Daron.

Fautenberry waived his right to a jury trial and entered a plea of "no contest" to the charges against him. In September 1992, a panel of three judges found Fautenberry guilty and sentenced him to death. He was executed by lethal injection on July 14, 2009.

Sean Vincent Gillis

Sean Vincent Gillis is a most unusual serial killer. Not only did he vary his murder methods, but the victims he chose varied greatly in age, while they were also not defined by race, as is typical. Then there were his long cooling off periods between crimes, set against spells of frantic activity. Finally, when another serial killer appeared on his patch, Gillis observed the case with interest, then set out to outdo his rival.

The first victim attributed to Gillis was 82-year-old Ann Bryan, stabbed to death in her apartment on March 21, 1994. Investigators believe that Gillis entered Mrs. Bryan's home with the intention of raping the elderly woman. However, when she woke and started screaming, he cut her throat, then stabbed and slashed at her body with a 12-inch hunting knife.

The murder of Ann Bryan would go unsolved until 2004. Meanwhile, Gillis lay fallow for five years before he struck again, killing a black drug addict and prostitute named Katherine Hall. Gillis picked Hall up on a chilly night in January 1999. Once he had her in his car, he overpowered her, then strangled her with a plastic cable tie. He then committed necrophilia with the corpse before mutilating it with his knife. The body was later found on a rural road in East Baton Rouge, Louisiana, placed (probably deliberately) beside a "Dead End" sign.

Four months later, in May 1999, Gillis was trolling for victims when he spotted 52-year-old Hardee Schmidt, out for a morning jog in an up-market South Baton Rouge suburb. Schmidt was a keen runner who jogged every day, giving Gillis the opportunity to observe her movements over the next three weeks. Eventually, on Sunday, May 30, he struck.

After knocking the victim over with his car, Gillis dragged her into a ditch and choked her into unconsciousness. He then dragged her to his vehicle and drove to a nearby park where he raped and murdered her. After mutilating the corpse with a knife, he loaded it into the trunk of his car, where it remained overnight. The following day he drove to St. James Parish, about 35 miles from Baton Rouge and dumped the body. It was found the next day by a cyclist.

Over the next year, Gillis claimed three more victims. Joyce Williams, 36, was killed on November 12, 1999, one of her legs entirely severed from the body. Lillian Robinson, 52, was killed in January 2000, her naked corpse discovered by an angler a month later. Then, in late October 2000, he killed 38-year-old Marilyn Nevils, dumping her mutilated corpse beside the Mississippi River.

After the Nevils murder, Gillis went to ground and remained so for over a year. But then something happened to bring him out of "retirement." Another serial killer was working his turf. Not only that, but whereas most of Gillis' murders had gained scant media attention, this killer (who targeted wealthy, white women and colleague students) was front-page news. Even more irksome to Gillis, the press was calling this newcomer, "The Baton Rouge Killer."

The Baton Rouge Killer would eventually be apprehended in May 2003, having claimed 8 victims. He was a 34-year-old ex-convict named Derrick Todd Lee, a black man who, unusually, targeted white women.

Lee may have been in custody, but Sean Vincent Gillis was still at large and in October 2003, he killed again. The victim was Johnnie Mae Williams, a 45-year-old drug addict and prostitute. Gillis had known Williams for over 10 years, but that didn't stop him beating, raping and strangling her to death, before mutilating her body. He even posed the corpse afterwards and photographed it in various positions.

Gillis' eighth and final victim was 43-year-old Donna Bennett Johnston, killed in February 2004. Gillis picked up the extremely intoxicated prostitute, strangled her in his car and then drove her to a park where he had sex with the corpse before performing a series of bizarre mutilations. He then severed her left arm at the elbow and carried it from the scene. Later, he'd tell police that he'd used it as a masturbatory tool.

Gillis was eventually arrested in April 2004, after investigators matched tire tracks found at the Johnston dumpsite to his truck. He was subsequently linked by DNA evidence to several of his victims, while a search of his home produced a plethora of incriminating evidence. He was sentenced to life in prison without the possibility of parole in August 2007.

Sean Patrick Goble

Depending on who you asked, Sean Patrick Goble was either a "gentle giant," or a "very scary man." The 6-foot-3, 310-pound long-haul trucker, did indeed cut an intimidating figure. But those who knew him described a sensitive soul who was reduced to tears on hearing that his grandmother was ill. Another story doing the rounds was that Goble's girlfriend had once beaten him up. One thing that everyone agreed on, though, was that Goble fancied himself as a ladies' man, and talked ad nauseam about his exploits with women.

The story that would eventually bring Sean Goble to public attention began in January 1995, with the discovery of a female body along a stretch of Interstate-81, just north of Bristol, Virginia. Detective Kenneth L. Wilson got the call and arrived at the scene to find the strangled, partially clad corpse of a middle-aged woman. The body had been left in plain view. Her right leg had been severely mangled, having been run over by a vehicle, most likely an 18-wheeler.

There were few clues as to the victim's identity, although a taxicab receipt found in her pocket would eventually provide investigators with a name. She was Brenda Kay Hagy, a 45-year-old drifter with a rap sheet for prostitution and trespassing.

Another important find at the crime scene was a plastic bag, from which a clear thumbprint was lifted. However, any initial elation at this discovery was soon dampened when a request to the multi-state AFIS fingerprint system turned up nothing. Unperturbed, Wilson submitted the print to the FBI. The Feds promised to run it through their multiple systems but warned that a match could take up to a year.

While detectives waited to hear from the FBI, another body turned up on February 19. She was Sherry Masur, found wrapped in a blanket beside a road in Guilford County, North Carolina. She too had been strangled. Like the previous victim, Masur had a history of arrests for prostitution.

A month later, on March 19, the body of Rebecca Alice Hanes was discovered along I-81 in Tennessee, about 20 miles from where Brenda Kay Hagy had been found. The corpse was in similar condition to the others, strangled and partially clad. Like Brenda Hagy, she'd also been run over by a semi-trailer.

Detective Wilson and his team had meanwhile been busy, contacting other jurisdictions about similar homicides, interviewing truck drivers, and speaking to the families of the victims. None of these avenues got them any closer to the killer, although they did learn of a series of murders attributed to a trucker who went by the handle, "Stargazer." The elusive killer was said to drive a black Peterbilt rig and was linked to at least 10 victims.

Then, on May 30, 1995, Wilson finally got a break in his case when the FBI found a match to the fingerprint. It belonged to Sean Patrick Goble, a trucker who had been arrested in West Memphis, Arkansas, in September 1994 for creating a public disturbance with a prostitute. Further inquiries revealed that Goble was employed by Rocky Road Express, operating out of Winston-Salem, North Carolina.

On April 12, 1995, investigators called on the trucking company and requested access to their drivers' logs. The logs placed Goble in the vicinity of each of the murders at the time they'd occurred. "What type of rig does he drive?" Wilson asked the company owner. "A black Peterbilt," came the reply.

Goble was due back at base the following day and when he arrived, investigators were waiting for him. He initially denied any knowledge of the murders. However, once he was confronted with the fingerprint evidence, he immediately folded and admitted to killing Brenda Hagy, Sherry Masur, and Rebecca Hanes. He denied, however, that he was "Stargazer," steadfastly maintaining that he committed no more than the three murders he was charged with.

Sean Patrick Goble was sentenced to two consecutive life terms in Tennessee on December 15, 1995. He remains a suspect in numerous other unsolved murders.

Mark Goudeau

During the years 2005/2006, the city of Phoenix, Arizona, was plagued by two separate serial killers. The first of these, known as the "Serial Shooter," killed four and wounded at least 14 victims, in a series of drive-by shootings, which he described as "Random Recreational Violence." The other, who went by the pseudonym, "The Baseline Killer," was even more deadly, claiming nine victims in a series of shootings, centered on Baseline Road in South Phoenix. In addition, he committed a string of other crimes, 94 in all, including sexual assault, kidnapping, and robbery.

The one-man crime wave attributed to the Baseline Killer began on August 6, 2005, when three teenaged girls were forced behind a church near Baseline Road, and molested. Less than two weeks later, the same man assaulted and robbed another victim in the same area. On September 8, he went a step further, killing his first victim, an unnamed man, in the area of Mill Avenue, Tempe.

During September, he committed a number of sexual assaults, including an attack on two sisters in a Phoenix park. One of the women was visibly pregnant and the assailant exploited this, holding a gun to her belly while he raped her sister.

On November 3, 2005, a man with dreadlocks, wearing a fisherman's hat, held up a store on North 32nd Street, netting $720. Ten minutes later, the same man abducted a woman from a nearby parking lot and sexually assaulted her in her car. Four days later, three restaurants along the same road were robbed in quick succession.

The police were by now certain that they were searching for a single perpetrator. On December 12, they had another murder to deal with. Tina Washington, 39, was on her way home from the preschool where she worked when she was shot. A witness reported a man with a drawn gun standing over her body.

On February 20, 2006, the bodies of 38-year-old Romelia Vargas and 34-year-old Mirna Palma-Roman were found shot to death inside their snack truck at 91st Avenue. And another double homicide was discovered on March 16. Restaurant workers, Liliana Sanchez-Cabrera and Chao Chou, were found in the parking lot of a fast-food restaurant. Both had been shot in the head.

On April 5, 2006, a business owner investigating a foul smell behind his premises on North 24th Street, discovered the badly decomposed body of Kristin Gibbons. Like the other victims, she'd died of a head wound.

The police had to do something and on May 5, 2006, after yet another sexual assault, they went public with a list of 18 crimes attributed to the Baseline Killer. They also released a composite sketch of the killer, but it did nothing to stem the violence. On June 29, Carmen Miranda, 37, was abducted from a self-service carwash. She was found dead, with a gunshot wound to the head, just 100 yards away.

On September 4, Phoenix police announced an arrest in the 2005 attack on the woman and her pregnant sister. The suspect was a 42-year-old construction worker named Mark Goudeau. He was currently on parole, having served 13 years for a 1990 aggravated assault. Goudeau had a long rap sheet that included numerous arrests for rape. He'd been linked via DNA evidence to the attack.

Mark Goudeau was convicted of sexual assault in September 2007 and sentenced to 438 years in prison. On November 30, 2011, he was sentenced to death for the Baseline murders.

Despite strong ballistic, forensic, and DNA evidence, Goudeau continues to protest his innocence. It has not escaped the attention of investigators, however, that the Baseline attacks stopped abruptly after Goudeau was arrested.

Vaughn Greenwood

Criminal profilers, such as those employed by the FBI's Behavioral Sciences Unit, have attained near mythic status in the public perception, and with good reason too. Their criminal profiles have helped bring countless dangerous criminals to book, no doubt saving many lives in the process. There are, however, cases where the profile hinders rather than helps the situation. Once such instance was the hunt for the "Skid Row Slasher."

The Slasher's first known victim was David Russell, a transient found stabbed to death on the steps of the Los Angeles public library on November 13, 1964. The following day, the killer struck again, slashing and stabbing 67-year-old Benjamin Hornberg, in the restroom of a seedy hotel.

The police were sure that the two murders were connected, but with no concrete leads, the trail soon went cold and detectives moved on to more pressing cases. Then, more than a decade later, the Slasher was back, emerging on December 1, 1974, to kill 46-year-old Charles Jackson. The alcoholic drifter was slain on the exact spot where David Russell had died 10 years earlier.

A week later he struck again, knifing 47-year-old Moses Yakanac to death in a Skid Row alley on December 8. Arthur Dahlstedt, 54, was killed in an abandoned building three days later, and on December 22, 42-year-old David Perez was found stabbed to death in shrubbery adjacent to the LA public library, a favorite dumping ground for the killer.

The police barely had time to open a case file when another down-and-out, 58-year-old Casimir Strawinski, was found dead in his hotel room on January 9. The next to die was 46-year-old Robert Shannahan, found dead by a hotel maid with a bayonet protruding from his chest. The final Skid Row victim was 49-year-old Samuel Suarez, discovered in a seedy hotel room on January 17.

With the police swarming all over his favored hunting ground, the killer switched his attention to Hollywood. On January 29, 1975, he stabbed 45-year-old George Frias to death in his own apartment. Two days later, he struck again, killing and mutilating 34-year-old Clyde Hays in his Hollywood home.

Criminal profiling at this time was not commonly in use as an investigative technique. However, with a brutal series of mutilation murders on their hands and not much to go on, the

LAPD decided to commission a psychiatric profile. They also took the ill-advised step of publishing their findings, something that would come back to embarrass them before long.

The profile described the Slasher as a white male in his late twenties or early thirties, six feet tall, 190 pounds, with shoulder-length blond hair. He was further described as sexually impotent with feelings of inadequacy, a friendless, poorly educated loner, who was probably homosexual and had an unspecified physical deformity.

On February 2, William Graham was attacked in his Hollywood home by a hatchet-wielding prowler. Fortunately for Graham, his houseguest, Kenneth Richer, came to the rescue. In the struggle that ensued, both men crashed through a plate-glass window, at which the attacker fled. His escape route led him past the home of actor Burt Reynolds, where he carelessly dropped a letter bearing his name, in the driveway.

Police made an arrest soon after. The suspect was 32-year-old Vaughn Orrin Greenwood and contrary to their profile he was a black man with no obvious deformities. Greenwood was a loner and a homosexual, but there was no evidence that he was impotent.

Originally from Pennsylvania, Greenwood had spent most of his adult life drifting between Chicago and the West Coast. He'd pulled a five-year jail term for aggravated battery in Chicago in 1966, which partially explained the decade-long gap between murders two and three.

Greenwood was convicted on nine counts of first-degree murder on December 30, 1976. He was sentenced to life in prison, with the recommendation that he should never be released.

William Hance

Between September 1977 and April 1978, the city of Columbus, Georgia, was plagued by a series of horrendous rape-murders. The killer would ultimately be identified as Carlton Gary, a black serial slayer known as the "Stocking Strangler." Six elderly, white women would lose their lives before Gary was brought to justice. The city would be thrown into such and uproar that another brutal murder, committed in early September, passed almost unnoticed.

On September 6, 1977, the nude body of 24-year-old army private, Karen Hickman, was found near the women's barracks at Fort Benning. She'd been bludgeoned with a blunt instrument, then apparently run over several times with a motor vehicle. The murder had occurred elsewhere, and the body had subsequently been transported to an area where it was certain to be discovered.

A month after the murder, the police received an anonymous call directing them to where Hickman's clothes could be found. Investigators had since learned that the victim had lived a promiscuous lifestyle and had favored picking up black soldiers in bars. Her death, they decided, was more than likely the result of a date gone bad, an isolated crime that was unlikely to be repeated. They'd soon be proven wrong on that score.

On March 3, 1978, the Columbus chief of police received a letter, purportedly from a white supremacist group called the "Forces of Evil." It demanded the capture of the Stocking Strangler, threatening violence if this did not happen.

"Since that coroner said the Strangler is black," the note read, "we decided to come here and try to catch him or put more pressure on you. From now on black women in Columbus, Georgia, will be disappearing if the Strangler is not caught."

The letter went on to state that a local black woman, named Gail Jackson, had already been abducted and that she would be killed if the Stocking Strangler was not caught by June 1. Two more blacks would be killed if the murderer was still at large on September 1, the note went on.

Police were convinced the letter was a hoax, especially as no one named Gail Jackson had been reported missing in Columbus. But as their investigations continued, they discovered that a black prostitute, Brenda Gail Faison, had disappeared from a local tavern on February 28. Could this be the hostage the letter was referring to?

While investigators were still mulling that possibility, a second letter arrived on March 13. The writer now suggested that a ransom of $10,000 might secure the hostage's release.

Two weeks later, a third note arrived, claiming that another hostage, named Irene, had been abducted and was scheduled to die on June 1 if the Stocking Strangler case was not resolved. This note was written on military stationary, leading detectives to speculate that the writer might be a soldier stationed at Fort Benning.

And they soon had a lead on the woman the letter referred to. 32-year-old Irene Thirkield had gone missing on March 16, last seen in the company of an unnamed black soldier.

In the early hours of March 30, 1978, an anonymous caller directed MPs to a shallow grave just outside the military base. In it, they found the remains of Brenda Faison, her skull shattered and her face beaten to a bloody pulp. Four days later, another call, this time to the police, led to Irene Thirkield's headless corpse, hidden behind a pile of logs on the army base.

On April 4, military police asked a number of officers to review tape recordings of the anonymous phone calls. One of the officers recognized the voice as that of 26-year-old Private William Hance, an ammunition handler in the 10th Artillery.

Hance was arrested that same day and soon after confessed to the murders of Faison, Thirkield, and Karen Hickman. He later recanted his confessions, but a civilian jury found him guilty anyway. He was sentenced to death, sentence carried out in Georgia's electric chair on March 31, 1994.

Michael Hughes

In the late eighties and early nineties, the LAPD was struggling to deal with a near epidemic of crack cocaine usage in Los Angeles. As the number of users of this cheap and highly addictive drug ballooned out of control, police officers found themselves swamped by a deluge of associated problems - overdoses, gang warfare, street crime, and prostitution. It was also a time when L.A.'s murder rate climbed to unprecedented levels, peaking in 1992 at over 1,000.

Among the homicide victims were a disproportionately high number of drug-addicted women and, for a time, the police believed that an extremely prolific serial killer was at work. They dubbed this man the "Southside Slayer" and formed a task force, comprising LAPD officers and deputies from various Sherriff's departments, in order to catch him.

As it turned out, the Southside Slayer was a fiction and the crimes had numerous perpetrators, including several serial killers. One of those was Chester Turner, the infamous "Figueroa Corridor Killer," who murdered at least 10 women in an 11-year reign of terror. Another was Michael Hughes.

Hughes, a security guard, was originally arrested for four murders, committed between September 1992 and November 1993. The first of those was the killing of 26-year-old Teresa Ballard, whose partially clothed body was discovered in Jesse Owens County Park, near Century Boulevard, on September 23.

Over the next year, three more bodies would turn up, Brenda Bradley, 38, Terri Myles, 33, and Jamie Harrington, 29. All had been found in alleyways surrounding commercial properties in Culver City, all had been raped and strangled and all were found with traces of cocaine in their bloodstreams.

As police focused their attention on individuals working near the sites where the bodies were found, one name came to the fore, security guard and former US Navy serviceman, Michael Hughes. Hughes was arrested by Culver City police in December 1993 and convicted of four murders in 1998. He was sentenced to life in prison. That should have been the end of the story.

However, in 2008, cold case detectives checking for DNA matches to unsolved homicides picked up a match to four murders committed between 1986 and 1993. These bore a striking resemblance to the crimes for which Hughes was convicted.

In January 1986, 15-year-old Yvonne Coleman disappeared after she left her boyfriend's house. Her strangled body was found in an Inglewood park. Four months later, on May 26, another 15-year-old, Verna Williams, was found raped and strangled in a stairwell. And on August 30, 1990, Deanna Wilson, 30, was found murdered in a garage in Los Angeles. The fourth victim was 32-year-old Deborah Jackson, killed on June 25, 1993, in the midst of the spree for which Hughes was currently incarcerated.

Hughes was arraigned for these crimes on August 6, 2008. Investigators also suspect that he may have been involved in other unsolved homicides. They have advised their colleagues in Michigan, San Diego, and Long Beach, to run his DNA against unsolved murders committed there. Hughes spent time in those locations while serving with the U.S. Navy.

Leslie Irvin

Sales of arms and ammunition had gone through the roof. A crazed shooter was on the loose, rampaging through Vanderburgh County, Indiana, in a campaign of unprecedented carnage. Already six people were dead, and the latest murder had been the most brutal of all, claiming three lives in an orgy of senseless violence.

The first murder attributed to the killer the media were calling "Mad Dog" occurred on December 2, 1954. Mary Holland, a 33-year-old expectant mother, ran a liquor store with her husband, Charles, on Bellemeade Avenue, Evansville. On the night of the murder, Charles Holland left his wife alone in the store so he could run some errands. He returned to find the place deserted. A search of the premises turned up Mary's body in the restroom, dead from a single bullet wound to the head. Her hands were tied behind her back.

On December 23, Wesley Kerr, 29, was found shot to death at the gas station where he worked the night shift. There were a number of similarities to the Holland murder. The victim was found in a restroom, hands bound, killed by a gunshot to his head. The cash register was empty, the killer having gained $68.11 from the crime.

The police were almost certain that the same gunman was responsible for both murders and the press soon picked up on that theme. A reward of $1000 was offered by local newspapers for the capture of the killer, but just as suddenly as he'd appeared, the murderer dropped out of sight.

He resurfaced three months later, on March 21, 1955. John Ray Sailer, 7, arrived home from school to find his mother shot dead on their Posey county farm. Wilhelmina Sailer's hands were bound behind her back. A bullet to the head had ended her life.

A week later, in nearby Henderson County, Kentucky, a farmer named Goebel Duncan, his son, Raymond, and daughter-in-law, Elizabeth, were shot to death. Goebel's wife, Mamie, was also shot. She survived, albeit with the loss of her sight and no memory of the tragic event.

A number of clues came to light after this latest tragedy, most promisingly the sighting of a black sedan close to the crime scene on the day of the murders. This was described as having Indiana plates and accident damage to its left side.

The police now had what they believed was a description of the suspect's vehicle. Still, it took a stroke of luck to eventually bring the killer to justice.

On March 30, eight youths, all of them members of Evansville's Junior Sheriff Patrol, were driving along a road in the St. Joseph area northwest of Evansville. Spotting a black car parked at the side of the road, 18-year-old Bill Williams leaned out and shouted: "Hey, we're investigators." The black vehicle immediately sped away, but not before one of the youths jotted down the license number.

A check on the license plate turned up the name of Leslie Irvin, currently on parole from the Indiana State Prison where he'd served nine years for burglary. Irvin was pulled in for questioning and after he was found to be in possession of a wallet belonging to Wesley Kerr, he was charged with four murders. He soon confessed to two more.

The case generated massive publicity in Evansville and pursuant to a defense request for a change of venue was eventually moved to Princeton, Indiana. There, on December 20, 1955, the jury deliberated for just 90 minutes before finding Irvin guilty and recommending that he be executed in the electric chair.

While awaiting transfer to the Indiana State Prison, Irvin escaped. He was apprehended 20 days later in San Francisco, having reached that destination via Las Vegas and Los Angeles.

Irvin was returned to Indiana to await execution. However, with the date rapidly approaching, his attorneys got a stay after arguing that Irvin's trial had been prejudiced by media coverage of the case. Three further stays were granted before Irvin was given a new trial in June 1961. The verdict remained the same, but the sentence of the court this time was life in prison.

Leslie "Mad Dog" Irvin served his time at Indiana State Prison in Michigan City. He died there of lung cancer on November 9, 1983. He was 59 years old.

Philip Carl Jablonski

If ever there was ever anyone who disproves the notion that habitual murderers can be rehabilitated, it is 'Big Phil' Jablonski.

While doing time for the 1978 second-degree murder of his first wife, Melinda Kimball, Jablonski began casting around for pen pals, describing himself as a 'gentle giant,' who loved walking in the rain, romantic candlelight dinners, and teddy bears. How his correspondents squared this away with a man doing time for the brutal slaying of his nearest and dearest is open to conjecture. However, there were plenty of takers, and one of those, Carol Spadoni, would eventually become the second Mrs. Jablonski in 1982.

However, by the time Jablonski was released on parole in 1990, Carol was having serious doubts about her choice of husband. The big, sullen man frightened her and she told his parole officer that she did not want him anywhere near the Burlingame, California, home she shared with her elderly mother, Eva Petersen.

An uneasy truce ensued between the couple, during which time Jablonski found himself an apartment and attended a community college in Indio, California – a condition of his parole.

No one knows what triggered the explosion of violence that happened next. More than likely, Jablonski had been brewing on the rejection by his wife for some time and eventually snapped.

On April 22, 1991, he kidnapped Fathyma Vann, a 38-year-old, widowed mother of two, who attended classes with him. Driving her out to the Indio desert, he raped and then shot the woman, leaving her body in a ditch with the words "I Love Jesus" carved into her back. There were other mutilations too. Vann's ears were cut off and her eyes had been pried out of their sockets and removed from the scene.

The following day, April 23, Jablonski showed up at his estranged wife's home where he attacked her and her mother. Carol Jablonski was shot, suffocated with duct tape, and stabbed; 72-year-old Eva Petersen was raped and then shot to death.

Jablonski fled east, stopping on April 27 at a Utah truck stop, where he shot 58-year-old Margie Rogers to death during a robbery. He was arrested the following day, in Kansas. In his possession, police found a tape recording, in which he talks with relish about the murders of his wife and mother-in-law, as well as those of Vann and Rogers.

Jablonski went on trial in 1994, with prosecutors determined to seek the death penalty. To this extent, they presented evidence showing his history of violence, which included assaults and rapes on at least ten women, among them his first wife, his sister, his mother, and a girlfriend with whom he had a child. The defense countered by claiming diminished responsibility, citing abuse suffered at the hands of his alcoholic, gun-totting father, and his traumatic experiences in Vietnam.

In the end, the jury came down on the prosecution's side, ruling that Jablonski was legally sane at the time of the murders and recommending that he be put to death. The judge duly formalized the sentence, ordering Jablonski to be held on San Quentin's death row until his execution.

While awaiting his date with the needle, Phil Jablonski continues to trawl for male and female pen pals, introducing himself in his letters as, "Death Row Teddy."

Calvin Jackson

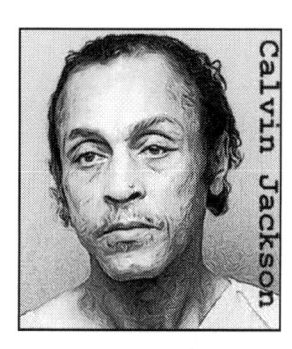

Despite its grandiose name, the Park Plaza Hotel on Manhattan's West 77th Street was a fleabag hostelry in an area that had known better days. It catered mainly to down-at-heel, middle-aged and older women, many of them on benefits. Between April 1973 and September 1974, it was also the scene of a series of brutal murders.

The first victim was 39-year-old resident Theresa Jordan, raped and strangled in her tiny room on April 10, 1973. The obvious motive was robbery, as the place had clearly been ransacked.

Three months later, on July 19, the killer struck again, tying 65-year-old Kate Lewisohn to her bed, raping and then strangling her, before caving in her skull with some heavy object. The apartment was also looted.

With frightened residents now in an uproar, the police threw some resources at the case before giving up due to lack of evidence. At any rate, it seemed the killer had moved on, if indeed the murders had been committed by the same man.

Nine months later, on April 24, 1974, another Park Plaza resident was killed, although the death of 60-year-old Mable Hartmeyer was at first put down to arteriosclerosis. It was only after someone noticed items missing from her room that an autopsy was called for. It revealed that Mrs. Hartmeyer had been raped and strangled.

The killer waited just four days before striking again. Yetta Vishnefsky, aged 79, was found dead in her room on April 28. She'd been tied up with nylon stockings, raped, and then stabbed to death. A butcher's knife was still buried to the hilt in her back when she was found. Items of clothing and jewelry, as well as a television set, were missing from her room.

By now, the tenants of the Park Plaza were desperate and terrified. They felt as though they'd been abandoned by the authorities. And with good reason too. With four murders spaced so closely together, you'd have thought the police would have been swarming all over the building. Except they weren't. It was hardly the NYPD's finest hour.

Winifred Miller, 47, died on June 8, raped, and then strangled to death. Eleven days later, Blanche Vincent, 71, was suffocated and raped in her room, her death initially attributed to alcoholism. Sixty-nine year old Martha Carpenter was suffocated and raped on July 1. Eleanor Platt, 64, followed her to the grave on August 30.

Her death was marked as "suspicious, cause unknown." Autopsy results confirmed that she had been suffocated and raped after death.

Eight women had now died, killed for their meager possessions, radios, and ancient TV sets worth no more than a hundred dollars a piece. And yet the police were totally flummoxed. It would take a change of M.O. by the murderer to eventually bring matters to a head.

On the morning of September 12, 1974, 59-year-old Pauline Spanierman was found dead in her apartment, raped and strangled, her television missing. This murder did not happen at the Park Plaza, but in a building a block away, on West 77th Street.

In the course of making their inquiries, the police heard about a man seen lugging a television set up the fire escape in the early morning hours. Detectives then conducted a door-to-door search and found the missing set in an apartment where one Calvin Jackson was staying as a houseguest of the tenant. Jackson was known to the officers as a drug addict, mugger, and petty thief. He'd most recently served time for burglary, which coincided with the 9-month break in the Park Plaza murders.

Jackson was taken into custody after police learned that he was currently employed as a janitor at the Park Plaza Hotel. Under interrogation, he quickly confessed to the murders. The crimes had been committed to feed his drug habit, he said, but he'd also lingered in each victim's apartment, eating food from their refrigerators, and having sex with their corpses.

Jackson was eventually convicted of a catalog of crimes and handed a mammoth sentence of 18 consecutive life terms. With time off for good behavior, he could theoretically be eligible for parole in 2030, when he will be 82 years old.

Milton Johnson

Milton Johnson was just 19 years old when he committed his first serious crime, the rape and torture of a Joliet, Illinois, woman, which earned him a prison term of 25 to 35 years. That sentence should have seen him confined until at least 1986, but the parole board saw fit to release Johnson three years early. Their generosity would cost at least ten, and possibly as many as 18, lives.

Who knows what was going through Milt Johnson's mind when he walked free from prison on March 10, 1983. The promise of a new life? A new beginning? Whatever it was, he must have found the world he'd left behind 13 years earlier, not to his liking. How else can you explain the carnage he unleashed during two blood-soaked months between June 25 and August 25, 1983?

The killing spree began with the murder of two sisters in Will County on Saturday, June 25. A week later, on July 2, Kenneth and Terri Johnson were shot to death in an apparently motiveless double homicide. Two weeks passed. Then, on Saturday, July 16, the killer carried out his bloodiest spree yet, killing five people in a single night, including two sheriff's deputies.

The following evening, 18-year-old Anthony Hackett was shot dead as he sat in his car. His fiancée, Patricia Payne, was forced from the vehicle into a pickup truck and driven from the scene by the African-American assailant. After leaving the interstate the man drove Payne to a remote location where he raped her before stabbing her in the chest and leaving her for dead. Fortunately, she was found by a passing motorist an hour later and was rushed to a Joliet hospital where doctors were able to save her life.

After the Hackett murder, the killer lay low. He returned with a vengeance a month later, hacking and shooting four women to death in a Joliet pottery shop. Proprietor Marilyn Baers, 46, and her three customers, Anna Ryan, 75; Pamela Ryan, 29; and Barbara Dunbar, 39, died at the scene.

The following evening, he shifted his killing ground to Park Forest, in Cook County, where he tied up 40-year-old Ralph Dixon and 25-year-old Crystal Knight before slashing their throats, additionally stabbing the female victim 20 times.

By now the police knew that the killer carried out his murderous campaigns over weekends, and the press had dubbed the unknown assailant "The Weekend Murderer." But he broke his pattern with the next murder, killing 82-year-old Anna Johnson on Thursday, August 25, and bringing the death toll to 17.

And yet the police had very little to go on. They knew, from Patricia Payne's testimony that they were hunting an African American man. But Payne had been unable to identify her assailant after three mug shot lineups. With very little else to go on, all investigators could do was pray for some lead to appear.

It eventually came on March 6, 1984, when a woman named Ann Shoemaker telephoned the Will County sheriff's office and described an incident that had happened in July 1983. She and a friend had been driving in Joliet when they noticed a truck that appeared to be following them. After the truck made several passes, Shoemaker jotted down the license plate number, but the vehicle drove off and she later dismissed the incident.

Now she passed the license number on to police who found that the truck belonged to Sam Myers, and was often used by his stepson, an ex-con named Milton Johnson. A search of the vehicle turned up a wealth of evidence including hair that matched Patricia Payne, bloodstains, and a sales receipt for a Tasmanian Devil stuffed doll that Anthony Hackett had bought for his fiancée on the day of his murder.

Milton Johnson was arrested while visiting his parole officer on March 9, 1984. He was eventually charged with 10 murders and sentenced to death. He currently awaits execution on death row at Joliet, Illinois, the scene of his murderous spree.

Vincent Johnson

DNA technology has been a boon for homicide investigators the world over, allowing them to resolve countless investigations. Equally important, though, is the role played by DNA in absolving innocent suspects of wrongdoing. In the case of the "Brooklyn Strangler," the benefits of DNA technology were seen in both these capacities.

The Strangler first announced his deadly presence with the August 1999 murder of 26-year-old Vivian Caraballo, found strangled with a piece of cloth on the roof of a building in Williamsburg, New York. Three weeks later, on Sept. 16, another strangled corpse was discovered. Joann Feliciano, 35, had been throttled with a sneaker lace and left on the roof of another apartment building. The next victim was found strangled to death inside her own apartment in Bedford-Stuyvesant. Rhonda Tucker was just 21 years old when she died on September 25, 1999.

A little more than a week after the Tucker murder, the body of Katrina Niles, 34, was found in her apartment on Marcy Avenue in Bedford-Stuyvesant. She'd been strangled with an electrical cord and her throat had been slashed.

Four months passed before the killer struck again. In January 2000, firefighters responded to reports of a blaze underneath the Williamsburg Bridge approach ramp and found the body of Laura Nusser, 43. She'd been strangled with an electrical cord.

The final victim was Patricia Sullivan, 48, found strangled to death with her own sneaker laces on June 22. Her body was dumped in a vacant lot on Marcy Avenue, Williamsburg.

The police by this time had a suspect in the murders, a 42-year-old homeless man who was known to associate with prostitutes in the areas where the bodies had been found. The man was pulled in for questioning and voluntarily submitted to a DNA swab, which investigators immediately sent for comparison with evidence taken from the victims.

Given the willingness with which the man agreed to provide the sample, detectives immediately suspected that they had the wrong man, and so it proved when DNA testing definitively eliminated him as the killer.

The man did, however, have something to share with the task force officers. He said that he knew the identity of the killer, another homeless man in the area, with whom he frequently used crack cocaine. According to the informant, the man that police should be looking for was Vincent Johnson, a homeless crack addict who stood just 5-foot-three and weighed in at a puny 130 pounds.

The detectives were at first skeptical that the diminutive Johnson was the brutal strangler they sought, but their informant was adamant. Johnson, he said, was obsessed with sadomasochistic sex and had admitted to having sex with two of the slain women.

Johnson was brought in for questioning in August 2000. He insisted that he knew nothing of the murders and did not know the victims. When asked to provide a DNA sample, he flatly refused. With no evidence to hold him, the police were forced to cut him loose.

Then one of the officers who had brought Johnson in for questioning recalled seeing Johnson spit in the street shortly before entering the precinct building. The officer had cautioned him about it at the time and was now able to collect a sample, which was sent for analysis. It provided the police with the DNA match they needed.

Confronted with the DNA evidence, Johnson confessed to the murders of six women: Patricia Sullivan, Rhonda Tucker, Joanne Feliciano, Elizabeth Tuppeny, Vivian Caraballo and Laura Nusser. He remains a suspect in the murder of Katrina Niles, although, he denies involvement in her death.

50 American Monsters You've Probably Never Heard Of Volume 2

On March 10, 2001, Vincent Johnson was sentenced to life in prison without the possibility of parole.

Roger Kibbe

The freeways and bi-ways of southern California have produced more than their fair share of roaming serial killers. Some, like the unholy trinity of Patrick Kearney, William Bonin, and Randy Kraft, have achieved lasting infamy within the annals of serial murder. Others, Roger Kibbe, for example, are less well known. Yet the 1-5 Strangler was every bit as depraved as the trio mentioned above, if slightly less prolific.

Kibbe committed his first known homicide in 1977, the September 15 rape and murder of 21-year-old Lou Ellen Burleigh. Thereafter, he apparently went back to his life as a hen-pecked husband who earned his living as a furniture maker and got his kicks skydiving at the weekends. Eventually, though, the murderous side of Roger Kibbe re-emerged and he took to cruising the highways for new prey, killing at least six young women between 1986 and 1987.

Kibbe's methodology was simplicity itself. He'd drive until he spotted a potential victim broken down at the side of the road. Playing the knight in shining armor, he'd offer to help, lulling his victim into a false sense of security before he struck. With the woman under his control, he'd drive her to a remote spot, where he'd rape, assault, and eventually strangle her with her own clothing. He'd then dump the body along an isolated stretch of Interstate-5 and drive away.

The first victim killed in this way was 21-year-old Lora Heedrick. Lora had last been seen getting into her car in her hometown of Modesto, California, on April 21, 1986. Her whereabouts would remain a mystery until her decomposed corpse was found near the intersection of Highway 12 and I-5 on September 6, 1986.

Barbara Ann Scott, 29, was killed on July 3, 1986, her brutalized corpse dumped beside I-5. Less than 2 weeks later, 19-year-old Sacramento native, Stephanie Brown, was discovered in a ditch beside Highway 12 near Terminus Island. She had been strangled and sexually assaulted. A crumpled map was found beside her car, which was parked alongside Interstate 5.

On August 17, Charmaine Sabrah, 26, was driving to her home in Sacramento when her car broke down at Peltier Road and Interstate 5. A man in a two-seat sports car pulled over and offered assistance. Leaving her mother with the disabled vehicle, Charmaine left with the man in order to get help. She was never seen alive again. Her strangled body was found near Highway 124 in Amador County on November 9, 1986.

Shortly before that discovery, another strangled corpse was found discarded beside the highway - that of 25-year-old Katherine Kelly Quinones.

The murder that would eventually trip Kibbe up was that of 17-year-old prostitute Darcie Frackenpohl. The runaway from Seattle was killed after she disappeared from a West Sacramento street. Her naked body was found in the mountains south of Lake Tahoe in 1987. Nylon fibers found on Darcie's body were from a type of rope used specifically in skydiving. Following that line of inquiry led task force investigators eventually to Kibbe.

Kibbe was convicted of the Frackenpohl murder and given a sentence of 25 years to life. And he must have thought he'd gotten off lightly, with the prospect of parole not ruled out.

Investigators knew, of course, that Kibbe was involved in at least three of the other I-5 murders. Similar rope fibers had been found at those crime scenes and Kibbe had not exactly been discreet about the crimes, mouthing off to other prisoners about his exploits. There were even true crime books written in the 1990s that named him as the prime suspect.

However, given that the victims had been discovered in different counties, trying him for those crimes represented a logistical and legal nightmare. It was only once California law was changed to allow one county to prosecute crimes from several jurisdictions that the prosecution could move ahead.

Kibbe was indicted on six charges of capital murder in February 2008. Given the very real prospect of the death penalty, he made a deal confessing to the murders in exchange for life in prison. He was duly sentenced to six consecutive life terms on November 4, 2009. Investigators suspect his involvement in as many as 38 unsolved homicides.

Tillie Klimek

Born Otillie Gburek in Poland in 1876, Tillie Klimek came to the United States with her parents as an infant. The family settled amongst the large Polish community on Chicago's Near North Side, where Tillie grew to be a rather squat, plain looking girl. She had no shortage of suitors, though, and in 1892, married her first husband, John Mitkiewicz.

The couple appeared happily married and would remain so for over 20 years. Then, in 1914, Tillie suddenly became afflicted with visions. She told a friend that she had dreamed of her husband's death, even naming the day on which he would die. Sure enough, John Mitkiewicz soon fell ill and died on the exact date that Tillie had predicted. She set aside her grief just long enough to call on the insurance company to collect on John's life policy.

Tillie was now a forty-year-old widow, and time had not improved her looks. Still, she wasn't alone for long. Within two months of Mitkiewicz's death, she'd married a laborer named John Ruskowski. Sadly, Ruskowski (the picture of health before he married Tillie) soon succumbed to illness. Within six months, Tillie's prediction of his impending death was realized.

Frank Kupszcyk was next and lasted barely as long as his predecessor. His death contributed both to Tillie's bank balance and to her burgeoning reputation as a 'psychic.'

Within a year, Tillie was wed and widowed again. Husband number four, Joseph Guszkowski, had scoffed at her predictions of his imminent demise, even when she'd bought a budget coffin in advance and sat by his bedside knitting a bonnet for the funeral.

Tillie's predictions of death had by now earned her an ominous reputation. People would cross the street when they saw her coming, not wanting to hear about their own deaths. Their fears were not without foundation. Aside from the four husbands she'd already dispatched, other people in Tillie's circle were dying too. Three members of a family she'd quarreled with had died in agony after she'd predicted their deaths; an ex-boyfriend, Joseph Grantkowski, had died after jilting her; four of Tillie's cousins had expired after being attended by her; several members of the Koulik family – into which Tillie's cousin Nellie had married – had become ill and succumbed to mysterious ailments. There were others too, usually people who'd annoyed Tillie in some or other minor way, or from whose death she could benefit.

With all of this going on, it is a wonder that she was still able to attract suitors, but she was. Next up was Anton Klimek, who proposed to Tillie in 1921, over the objections of his family. No sooner had the ink dried on his will (bequeathing all of his worldly possessions to Tillie), than Anton was struck down by illness.

This time, however, Tillie's in-laws were prepared, and they swiftly arrived to transport Anton to hospital, where he made a full recovery. The cause of his mystery illness was also revealed. He'd been fed copious amounts of arsenic.

The hospital notified the police department and in short order, Tillie was under arrest, along with her cousin Nellie. An exhumation of her former husbands proved that they too had been poisoned.

Tillie Klimek stood trial in March 1923, for the murder of Frank Kupzsyk, her third husband. She was sentenced to life in prison and remained incarcerated until her death on November 20, 1936.

Nellie Koulik spent a year in prison before being acquitted of all charges.

Timothy Krajcir

Timothy Krajcir was born in the small town of Laury's Station, Pennsylvania on November 28, 1944. Abandoned by his father at birth, he was raised by a mother he described as cold and unaffectionate. He'd later tell prison psychologists that he hated her.

Entering his teens, Timothy was a shy and introverted boy, obsessed with sexual fantasies but lacking the courage to approach girls his own age. Instead, he channeled his energy into voyeurism, becoming a compulsive peeping tom in the area where he lived.

After graduating high school, Krajcir spent a short time in the Navy. After his discharge in1963, he served his first jail term for sexual assault. This would set a pattern for the rest of his life. With the exception of two short periods in the late 1970s and early 1980s, Krajcir would spend his entire adult life in prison. Unfortunately, those brief periods of freedom would cost at least nine women their lives.

Krajcir's first known murders occurred in 1977. He'd just been released from his latest period of incarceration and decided to move to Carbondale in southern Illinois, where he got a job driving an ambulance. Krajcir enjoyed the work and loved the authority that the uniform bestowed upon him, providing, as it did, the perfect cover for the monster that lurked beneath.

Most serial killers target victims in areas that they are familiar with, but Krajcir was probably aware that he'd come under immediate suspicion for a murder committed in a small town like Carbondale. His solution was simple. He began spending all of his spare time cruising the neighboring towns, stalking potential victims, finding out where they lived then breaking in and lying in wait while they were out. His favorite locale was Cape Girardeau, Illinois. Between the years 1977 and 1982, he'd commit a series of brutal rape-murders here.

The first Cape Girardeau murders occurred in 1977, when the slayings of mother and daughter, Mary and Brenda Parsh, and later Sheila Cole, threw the small community into a state of panic before the murders abruptly stopped. They resumed five years later in 1982. Margie Call and Mildred Wallace were raped and murdered by a home-invading assailant, while Southern Illinois University student, Deborah Sheppard, died in similar circumstances.

The reason for the gap between the two killing sprees would later become all too clear. Krajcir had been sentenced to yet another prison term in 1979, this time for the statutory rape of a 13-year-old girl, the daughter of his landlord.

Following his release in 1982, Krajcir became the first resident of Jackson County, Illinois, to be designated a "sexually dangerous person." He was also required to undergo psychiatric treatment, and took classes in at SIU, eventually earning a degree in Administrative Justice with a minor in psychology.

However, none of these measures discouraged Krajcir from committing acts of violence against women. Six months after he murdered Mildred Wallace, he returned to Pennsylvania where he robbed a couple of women at gunpoint, then forced them to undress and fondle him. After another such incident the following year, Krajcir was arrested and charged with a catalog of crimes – theft, receiving stolen property, reckless endangerment, indecent exposure, criminal trespass, aggravated assault, indecent assault, and firearms violations.

The sentence was surprisingly light, just 5 years, to be served at Big Muddy River Correctional Center in Ina, Illinois. It was while serving this term that DNA evidence linked Krajcir to the Cape Girardeau murders.

Confronted with the evidence, and facing the prospect of the death penalty if convicted, Krajcir struck a deal and confessed. He also admitted to three additional murders; Virginia Lee Witte, 51, strangled and knifed to death on May 12, 1978; Joyce Tharp, 29, abducted from her home in 1979, killed in southern Illinois, then dumped in Paducah, Kentucky; and 51-year-old Myrtle Rupp, raped and killed in Reading, Pennsylvania, in 1979.

In 2008, Timothy Krajcir was sentenced to additional life terms in Illinois and Missouri. He is currently held at Tamms Correctional Facility in Illinois. He will never be released.

Peter Kudzinowski

Peter Kudzinowski was one of a trio of infamous child-killers who plagued the eastern seaboard during the early years of the 20th century (the others being Albert Fish and J. Frank Hickey). A native of Poland, Kudzinowski immigrated to the United States with his family as a child.

The family settled in Scranton, Pennsylvania, where Kudzinowski worked as a miner. He later moved to New Jersey where he found employment as a railroad worker. It was in New Jersey that two of the three murders attributed to him occurred.

Kudzinowski's first confessed murder was that of an adult man named Harry Quinn, killed in Scranton, Pennsylvania in 1924.

Four years later, on August 19, 1928, 5-year-old Julia Mlodzianowski was attending a school picnic at Lake Hopatcong, New Jersey, when Kudzinowski lured her into the woods nearby. After strangling the little girl he carried her body from the scene, later throwing it from a moving freight train into the Delaware River. Julia was never found.

Kudzinowski next surfaced in Manhattan, New York, on November 17, where he encountered 7-year-old Joseph Storella. Earlier in the day, Kudzinowski had tried to persuade two children, a boy and a girl, into "going to the pictures" with him, but they'd run away. Joseph was more agreeable, accompanying Kuzinowski to the movie, then traveling with him on the Port Authority Trans-Hudson train to Journal Square in Jersey City, New Jersey. From there, he took the young boy to a meadow, near Secaucus, New Jersey. When Joseph tried to escape, Kudzinowski knocked him down and punched him several times before slashing his throat. He then covered the body with the boy's overcoat and walked calmly away from the scene.

The disappearance of Joseph Storella created and uproar, causing Kudzinowski to flee to Detroit, Michigan, where he was later arrested. He was brought back to New Jersey and subjected to a brutal round of questioning, with even Jersey City mayor, Frank Hague, getting in on the act. Eventually, at the urging of his mother, Kudzinowski broke down and admitted to killing Joseph Storella, Julia Mlodzianowski, and Harry Quinn.

He went on trial for murder in November 1928, the jury taking just 63 minutes to find him guilty. Judge Egan then sentenced him to die in the electric chair. That sentence was carried out at the New Jersey State Prison in Trenton, on December 21, 1929.

Kudzinowski was also a suspect in a number of other high-profile child murders, including the murder of Billy Gaffney (Albert Fish later confessed to this crime), and Irving Pickelny, who disappeared from Brooklyn in February 1927.

DeVernon LeGrand

DeVernon LeGrand was an ordained minister. At least, that's what he told people. Then again, he also said that he had degrees in psychology and theology; he also said that he had never harmed anyone. None of it was true. "The Reverend" was in fact a pimp and a drug dealer, a serial rapist, and the murderer of at least four (and possibly as many as 25) people. And he concealed all of his activities behind the outwardly respectable façade of St. John's Pentecostal Church of Our Lord in Brooklyn, New York.

LeGrand was unlike any preacher you're familiar with. He cruised the streets of New York in a chauffeur-driven, cream-colored Cadillac, complete with its own bar and TV. He wore silk suits and had elaborately coiffured hair. He was charming and persuasive. Those young women who fell for his charms, though, soon saw another side of the reverend, an abusive control freak who used rape, drugs and intimidation to manipulate his flock. Those who he couldn't control simply vanished. Like his first wife, Ann Sorise, or his second wife, Ernestine Timmons, or 23 other parishioners, who went missing and were never seen or heard from again.

A native New Yorker, born in 1925, LeGrand founded his church in 1965. That same year he was arrested on charges of kidnapping, assault, and firearms possession.

His method of recruiting new members to his flock was simple. He'd cruise the streets looking for vulnerable young women who he'd charm with his slick line of talk and his show of wealth. Once under his spell, the gullible women were convinced to hit the streets dressed in the garb of nuns to collect money for the church. These collections (as well as sidelines in drugs and prostitution) netted LeGrand an estimated $250,000 a year, allowing him to live a movie star lifestyle. There were gambling trips to Atlantic City, tailored suits, expensive booze, and drugs. He also bought several properties, including a 58-acre farm in the Catskills, and a four-story townhouse at 222 Brooklyn Avenue, where the church was situated.

It was also here that LeGrand housed his harem of "nuns," in tiny bedrooms they shared with the 47 children he'd fathered by them. Those who tried to leave were threatened with their lives and the lives of their children. On more than one occasion, LeGrand followed through with his threats.

The double homicide that would eventually bring LeGrand's kingdom crashing down occurred in 1975. LeGrand and his son, Noconda, had been convicted of raping a 20-year-old woman in the church. Then two church members came forward to say that

LeGrand had murdered his daughter-in-law, Gladys Stewart, 18, because she wanted out of the family. (Gladys had also helped prosecutors convict LeGrand of rape, but he was unaware of this.)

On October 3, 1975, Gladys told LeGrand she was leaving. He then ordered the congregation to go to the downstairs meeting room, while he and another son, Steven, detained Gladys and her 16-year-old sister, Yvonne Rivera. Over the next two hours, the teens were subjected to a brutal beating. One of LeGrand's children, who crept upstairs to sneak a peek, returned to report that, "Daddy's stomping Gladys." When the congregation heard screaming from upstairs they drowned it out by singing hymns.

At around 2:30 in the morning, LeGrand finally allowed his flock to go to bed. Over the next two weeks, he openly bragged to his parishioners about killing and dismembering Gladys and her sister. He threatened them with the same if they disobeyed him.

Then, one day, he ordered church handyman, Frank Holman, to load two large garbage bags into his car, drive them to the farm and burn them. When Holman was unloading the bags, something spilled out. It was Yvonne Rivera's severed head.

Terrified, the man did what he was told, burning the remains in an old bathtub, then putting the ashes in a garbage can, and tossing them into a pond. He then drove back to New York, where he and his wife decided to go to the police. Later, crime scene investigators would recover two bucketfuls of bone fragments from the disposal site.

LeGrand and his stepson Steven were convicted of the double homicide and each sentenced to 25 to life. DeVernon LeGrand died in prison in 2006 at age 82.

As for the LeGrand "church," it is still going strong under the stewardship of LeGrand's son, Noconda, the convicted rapist.

Michael Lee Lockhart

"Executioner, the one who hides behind the door of darkness, I am ready. Go ahead and push down the plunger of poison to murder me in the name of justice. I forgive you, I love you."

These words formed part of a two-page "final statement" written by condemned murderer, Michael Lee Lockhart, shortly before his execution. Yet, in truth, Lockhart himself was the executioner, the perpetrator of three horrendous mutilation murders of teenaged girls and the brutal gunning down of a police officer. He bragged in prison about having committed "more than two dozen" killings.

Lockhart would eventually be executed by lethal injection for the murder of police officer Paul Hulsey Jr. in Beaumont, Texas, on March 22, 1988. Earlier in the day, Hulsey had spotted Lockhart driving a red Corvette. The officer's suspicions were aroused when Lockhart stopped at various locations to talk with known drug dealers. Hulsey then followed Lockhart to a motel. He'd learned in the interim that the Corvette was stolen. Approaching Lockhart in his motel room, Hulsey tried to arrest him. A scuffle ensued during which the police officer was shot twice - first in the arm, and then, execution-style, through the heart and lungs. Lockhart then fled the scene but was arrested while trying to escape in a cab.

The cop-killer was in custody, but as officers were about to learn, Lockhart was responsible for far more than just a single murder.

The crime spree that brought Michael Lockhart from Toledo, Ohio, to Beaumont, Texas, had started over fifteen months earlier, around Christmas, 1986. It carried the drifter through Wyoming, Florida, Missouri, Illinois, Indiana, Ohio, Texas, and Louisiana. During the course of that journey, Lockhart was responsible for numerous counts of grand theft auto, robbery, and rape. He also committed at least four murders.

On October 13, 1987, the body of 16-year-old Windy Gallagher was found by her sister in the bedroom of their home in Griffith, Indiana. She was nude from the waist down with her hands tied behind her back. Her bra was pushed up, exposing her breasts. She'd been stabbed 21 times, four deep wounds cutting into her neck, another 17 inflicted on her abdomen. Worse yet, her stomach had been torn open and her intestines pulled through the gaping wound. Bloody fingerprints left at the scene were later matched to Lockhart.

Three months later, on January 20, 1988, Lockhart surfaced in Land O'Lakes, Florida, where he attacked 14-year-old Jennifer

Colhouer, knocking her unconscious and raping her before launching another frenzied knife attack. As in the case of Windy Gallagher, he then eviscerated the victim, leaving her intestines exposed. DNA evidence would later tie Lockhart to this horrific crime.

Lockhart was subsequently linked forensically to the mutilation murder of a co-ed at Vincennes University, in Indiana.

During his trial for the murder of Paul Hulsey, Lockhart made a desperate bid for freedom, jumping from a third story courthouse window and sustaining injuries in the process. He was quickly recaptured and would eventually keep his date with the executioner on December 9, 1997.

Orville Lynn Majors

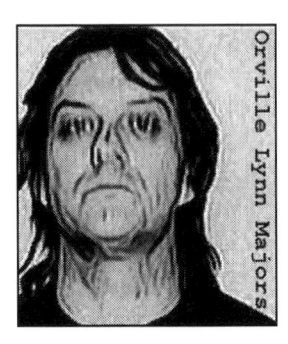

Nursing is a tough profession, which demands a lot of its practitioners. Those who take up the calling are faced daily with death and disease, long, physically demanding work hours and patients who can often be difficult and demanding. Quite aside from their technical qualifications, nurses require an abundance of patience, a natural empathy, and a genuine desire to serve their fellow man. The vast majority possess these qualities in abundance. Others, unfortunately, do not.

One has to wonder what it was exactly that attracted Orville Lynn Majors to the nursing profession. He seems to have been horribly unsuited to his chosen vocation, genuinely antagonistic towards the elderly patients under his care. One of the kinder epithets he applied to them was "waste." He also complained to acquaintances that the patients took pleasure in making his life difficult, that he hated their whining. They all deserved to be gassed, he said, although few would have guessed that he meant this literally.

Between the years 1993 and 1995, something was horribly wrong at the 56-bed Vermillion County Hospital in Clinton, Indiana. Death rates were off the scale, soaring from 26 in 1992 to 101 in 1994, most of them occurring in the 4-bed ICU. In the latter six months of 1994 alone, 67 people died. There were days when all four ICU patients expired.

Something clearly had to be done, and the hospital, therefore, brought in an expert to investigate. The consultant began by studying patient charts and nurses' time cards. Immediately, he picked up a pattern, something so glaringly obvious that it was a miracle no one had spotted it earlier. The majority of deaths at the hospital had a common denominator, ICU nurse, Orville Lynn Majors.

The escalation in the death rate at the hospital coincided almost exactly with the beginning of Majors' employment there. In the four prior years, no more than 31 patients had died in any single year. Then, over the 22 months that Majors worked there, 147 died in the ICU; 121 of them while Majors was on duty. In fact, patients were 43 times more likely to die on Majors' shift than on any other, the consultant determined.

This was not, of course, proof of any wrongdoing. However, it had to be reported to the authorities and the subsequent investigation soon firmed up the consultant's suspicions. First, a quantity of potassium chloride was found in Majors' possession. Then, a round of exhumations uncovered symptoms consistent with an overdose of that particular drug, which would cause a sudden rise in blood pressure before the patient's hearts suddenly stopped. Perhaps most tellingly, the death rate at the hospital suddenly normalized after Majors was suspended from his job in the wake of the investigation.

Orville Lynn Majors went on trial for murder in October 1999. Although he was suspected in as many as 130 murders he was tried with only seven; Mary Ann Alderson, 69; Dorothea Hixon, 80; Cecil Smith, 74; Luella Hopkins, 89; Margaret Hornick, 79; Freddie Wilson, 56; and Derek Maxwell, Sr., 64.

The jury would eventually find Majors guilty on six of those murders, while they remained deadlocked in the case of Cecil Smith, forcing Judge Ernest Yelton to declare a mistrial on that charge.

In the remaining charges, the judge imposed six 60-year sentences, a total of 360 years, to be served consecutively. Majors would have to serve 180 years before being eligible for parole.

Richard Marquette

A native of Portland, Oregon, Richard Marquette had his first brush with the law in June 1956, when he was arrested on a charge of attempted rape. However, after his victim declined to press charges, the 21-year-old Marquette was released, appearing on police radars again just over a year later in August 1957. This time, he held up a gas station, clubbing the clerk with a wrench for good measure. Tried and found guilty, Marquette served just 12 months of an 18-month sentence before securing an early release.

He headed back to Portland, where on June 5, 1961, he was seen drinking in a local tavern with a 23-year-old housewife named Joan Rae Caudle. Later that day, Caudle's husband reported her missing, saying she'd gone out shopping for Father's Day gifts and had failed to return.

On June 8, 1961, Portland Police received a phone call from a distraught woman who said that her dog had brought home a human foot in a paper bag. A search of the area surrounding the woman's house soon turned up other body parts, all neatly severed and bled dry. Fingerprints identified the remains as Joan Caudle and a witness at the bar put the police on the trail of Dick Marquette.

Their suspect, however, had fled the coop, leaving behind filleted slices of his victim in the refrigerator. A warrant was issued for Marquette's arrest, and when a massive manhunt failed to find him, Oregon Governor Mark Hatfield appealed to the FBI for help. In response, the agency took the unusual step of adding Marquette as an 11th name to the "Ten Most Wanted" list (the first time this had ever been done). Marquette was arrested in Santa Maria, California, the following day.

Once in custody, Marquette quickly confessed. According to him, he'd met Caudle in the bar and after a few drinks had taken her back to his house where they had consensual sex. Afterwards, they'd gotten drunk together and had argued. He'd then strangled Caudle to death. He'd dismembered her because he didn't have a car to get rid of the remains, he said, although he could offer no explanation for the human "steaks" in his refrigerator.

Marquette was found guilty of first-degree murder and sentenced to life in prison. He was released from that term in 1973, having served less than 12 years. Two more women would die due to the parole board's munificence.

In April 1975, a fisherman was shocked to discover human remains floating in a shallow marsh in Marion County, Oregon. The mutilated corpse was determined by police to be that of 37-year-old Betty Wilson, a destitute mother of 11 children, all of them now in foster care. Wilson had last been seen in the company of a man at a local nightclub. Based on eyewitness testimony, the police soon focused their investigation on Richard Marquette.

A search of Marquette's mobile home turned up several pieces of physical evidence tying him to the murder. Just 55 hours after the remains were found, Marquette found himself in police custody again. He confessed almost immediately, offering a similar story to the one he'd used in the Caudle murder; he and Wilson had had sex, then argued, and he'd then strangled and dismembered her.

Marquette went on trial in May 1975 and was sentenced to life imprisonment without the possibility of parole.

While in custody, he confessed to a third murder. According to Marquette, he picked up the unnamed woman in a bar, took her home for sex, then strangled and dismembered her.

It was a familiar story and investigators initially wondered if Marquette was telling it simply to add to his notoriety. Those ideas were dispelled when Marquette led detectives to two shallow graves where he had disposed of the remains. The head was never found and as Marquette did not know the woman's name, her identity remains a mystery.

Rhonda Bell Martin

Rhonda Bell Martin was an enigma, even to herself. The plump, bespectacled 49-year-old admitted to murdering six people – two husbands, three young daughters, and her mother – over an 18-year period from 1937 to 1955. Yet, asked for the motive behind the murders she was unable to provide one.

It certainly wasn't for the money, the paltry sums she earned in life insurance payouts was barely enough to cover the funeral expenses. Why then did Martin become a serial poisoner of those closest to her? Given what we know of serial killers today the answer is simple. She was driven by a compulsion to kill, one that she could neither resist nor fathom.

Ronald Martin was Rhonda's fifth husband, the 29-year-old son of her former spouse, Claude Carroll Martin, who had died of a mystery ailment just eight months previously. Now Ronald too was ill, and with strikingly similar symptoms. Fortunately, for Ronald, he did not follow his father to the grave. Instead, he was rushed to hospital, where he was discovered to have a high concentration of arsenic in his system. The poison had already robbed him of the use of his legs and although he pulled through, he'd remained paralyzed from the waist down for the rest of his life.

The source of the poison was no great mystery, and in fact, Ronald's illness provided an explanation for his father's mysterious death eight months earlier. Rhonda Martin, Ronald's wife and former stepmother, had poisoned both men.

In March 1956, Rhonda was brought in for questioning and quickly admitted to killing Claude Martin. She also confessed to the murders of her second husband George Garrett in 1939; her daughters, 3-year-old Emogene Garrett in 1937, Anna Carolyn Garrett, 6, in 1940; and Ellyn Elizabeth Garrett, 11, in 1943; as well as her mother, Mary Frances Gibbon, in 1944.

She further admitted poisoning her fifth husband, Ronald Martin, with the intention of killing him. She strenuously denied murdering two of her other children, even though their deaths occurred in similar circumstances to those she admitted.

Despite her confessions, Martin was tried only for the murder of Claude C. Martin. This was common practice in those days, giving the prosecution other cases to pursue in the event of an acquittal. As she had already admitted to poisoning Claude with rat poison poured into his food and coffee, her lawyers put up the only defense open to them – they pled insanity.

This was never likely to succeed. On June 5, 1956, the jury deliberated for three hours and 10 minutes before returning a guilty verdict. The judge then sentenced Rhonda to die in the electric chair.

Rhonda Bell Martin went to her death on October 11, 1957. A few minutes after midnight, she was strapped into the chair and asked if she had anything to say. She shook her head silently. The switch was then thrown, passing 2,200 volts of electricity through her body. Clutching her Bible in her left hand, Rhonda stiffened briefly, then went slack. A short while later she was pronounced dead, the last woman executed by the state of Alabama.

Martin bequeathed her body to medical science, leaving a note that read:

"I want my body to be given to some scientific institution to be used as they see fit, but especially to see if someone can find out why I committed the crimes I have committed.

"I can't understand it, for I had no reason whatsoever. There is definitely something wrong. Can't someone find it and save someone else the agony I have been through."

Winston Moseley

The murder of Catherine "Kitty" Genovese is unique in the annals of American crime. It is one of the few cases in which the victim's name has become more famous than that of her killer.

The reason that the Genovese murder became such a cause célèbre is because it so starkly illustrates human apathy. The original report of the murder, carried by the New York Times on March 14, 1964, was a somewhat sensationalized account, describing an attack on a young woman, watched by 38 witnesses who stood by and did nothing. The truth is somewhat different. Less than a dozen witnesses saw parts of the attack and many who did mistook it for a lover's quarrel or a drunken brawl. Nonetheless, if just one of those witnesses had picked up the phone and dialed the police, Kitty Genovese might have lived. Asked later why that hadn't taken action, many offered a stock response, "I didn't want to get involved."

On the night of March 13, 1964, 28-year-old Kitty Genovese was returning to her apartment in Queens, New York, from her job as a bar manager. Unbeknownst to Kitty, a man had followed her and as she parked her car and walked towards her building, he got out of his vehicle and pursued her on foot. She'd made it no more than a hundred feet when he caught up to her and stabbed her in the back. Kitty screamed, causing one of her neighbors to open a window and shout out at the attacker, who then fled.

Badly but not mortally wounded, Kitty staggered towards the foyer of her building and made it through the door before collapsing. Her attacker then returned to renew the attack, attempting to rape the stricken woman before stabbing her to death. He then fled the scene, taking her purse containing $49.

From the time of the initial stabbing, the attack had lasted 35 minutes. Only once it was over, did someone call the police. Officers and emergency personnel were on the scene within minutes. Kitty Genovese was rushed to hospital but was pronounced dead on arrival.

Six days after the murder, the police arrested Winston Moseley, a 29-year-old, African-American business machine operator. Moseley was married with two children, a homeowner with no prior police record. Asked why he had attacked Genovese he said that his motive was simply "to kill a woman." He also confessed to two more murders.

Barbara Kralik, 15, was stabbed to death in her home on July 20, 1963; Annie May Johnson, 24, was shot and then set alight on February 29, 1964, two weeks before the Genovese murder.

Winston Moseley would eventually stand trial for all three murders and be sentenced to death. However, the sentence was later reduced to life in prison on the grounds that he had not been allowed to enter evidence of reduced competency, during the sentencing phase.

In 1968, while being transported to a hospital in Buffalo, New York, Moseley overpowered a guard and beat him senseless before taking five hostages and going on the run. He was at liberty for two days, during which time he raped one of his captives. Returned to prison, he was later an active participant in the Attica riots.

Moseley remains in prison having been denied bail on several occasions. At his latest hearing, in March 2008, he offered this argument in support of his request for early release:

"For the victim, it's a one-time or one-hour or one-minute affair, but for the person who's caught, it's forever."

Louise Peete

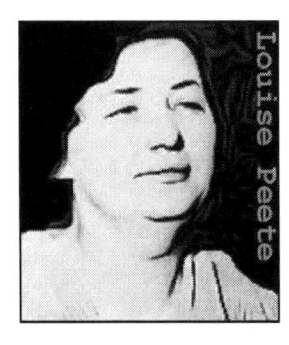

Louise Peete was born Lofie Louise Preslar, in Bienville, Louisiana, on September 20, 1880. The daughter of a wealthy newspaper publisher, she was educated at the best private schools in New Orleans. However, she soon developed a reputation for sexual promiscuity, leading to her eventual expulsion.

Back home in Bienville, Louise took up a life of leisure. In 1903, she married traveling salesman, Henry Bosley, and joined him on his travels. All went well until 1906, when Bosley arrived home to find his wife in bed with another man. Devastated by her infidelity, he killed himself two days later.

Louise next appeared in Boston, Massachusetts, where she worked as a high-class prostitute and supplemented her handsome earnings by stealing from her clients. Eventually caught at this game, she fled to Waco, Texas, where she wooed oilman Joe Appel, known for his extravagant diamond rings and diamond-studded belt buckles. One week after meeting Louise, Appel was dead from a bullet wound to the head and most of his jewelry was missing.

Louise was hauled before a grand jury. She pleaded self-defense, insisting that Appel had tried to rape her. So convincing was her performance that members of the jury actually applauded when she was set free. No questions were asked about the missing jewels.

By 1913, Louise was out of cash and down on her luck. She remedied the situation by marrying hotel clerk Harry Faurote in Dallas, Texas. For Louise, it was quite simply a marriage of convenience and the nuptials had barely been completed before she was openly carrying on affairs with other men. Driven to despair by his wife's infidelity, Faurote hung himself in the hotel basement.

The widow Faurote moved next to Denver, Colorado, where she married door-to-door salesman, Richard Peete in 1915. A year later, she bore him a daughter, but family life on a salesman's wage was not what Louise wanted. She abandoned her husband and child and took off for Los Angeles in 1920. There she became involved with Jacob Denton, a mining executive.

Louise wanted Denton to marry her, but he refused. It was a fatal mistake. Denton disappeared on May 30, 1920, and Louise took over his home, throwing a series of lavish parties. However, Denton's lawyer became suspicious of Louise's glib answers regarding his client's disappearance. He alerted the police and a search of the property turned up Denton's body, buried in the cellar. He'd been shot in the head.

As detectives launched a hunt for the missing "Mrs. Denton," Louise had already fled back to Denver, where she took up again with Richard Peete. She was eventually traced there and arrested.

Convicted of murder in January 1921, Louise was sentenced to life in prison. Richard Peete corresponded faithfully with her for years, but in 1924, after she refused to answer his letters, he became the third spouse of Louise Peete to take his own life. It is said that Louise boasted in prison about the husbands she had driven to kill themselves on her account.

Louise was eventually paroled in 1939 and found work at a serviceman's canteen. Soon after, an elderly co-worker disappeared, her home found ransacked. Louise had been friendly with the woman and was questioned about her disappearance, but the matter went no further.

In May 1944, she married an elderly bank manager named Lee Judson. Shortly after, Margaret Logan, Louise's guardian since her release, vanished. Louise told Margaret's elderly husband that his wife was in the hospital and not allowed to receive visitors. She then persuaded the authorities to confine the old man to a mental hospital where he died six months later. Louise then moved into the Logan house with her husband.

Louise continued to submit reports to her parole officer, ostensibly from Margaret Logan. But, by December 1944, the parole officer had become suspicious of the glowing updates and dubious signatures. He alerted the police and a search of the Logan home turned up Margaret Logan's body, buried in the garden with a bullet hole in the head.

Louise was placed under arrest, her husband booked as an accessory. He would eventually be acquitted on January 12, 1945. The following day, he threw himself from the 13th floor of a Los Angeles office building.

Louise meanwhile had been convicted of first-degree murder and sentenced to die. She was executed in San Quentin's gas chamber on April 11, 1947.

Steven Pennell

Delaware has had fewer serial killers than any other state in the Union, with only one documented case in the state's long history. That case first came to light in November 1986, when a vicious predator, known as "The Corridor Killer," began preying on the women of New Castle.

On November 29, 1986, the brutalized corpse of 27-year-old Shirley Ellis was found discarded beside Interstate 40. She'd been raped and strangled to death but that only told part of the story. Ellis had been sadistically tortured prior to death, the killer using various knives, pliers, needles and whips to torment her.

Over the next twelve months, four more women would share Ellis's horrendous fate before police closed in and arrested a suspect. He was Steven Brian Pennell, a seemingly normal, happily married electrician, with no criminal record. He had at one time been a criminology student.

Not much is known of Pennell's background except that he was a Delaware native, born in 1957, who harbored a burning desire to become a law enforcement officer. To this extent, he began a course in criminology at the University of Delaware, completing several semesters while applying to various state and county police departments. For whatever reasons, all of these applications were turned down, leading to Pennell abandoning his studies and pursuing a career as an electrician instead.

Whether those rejections had anything to do with the monster that would emerge later is unknown. Pennell settled in New Castle, married and got on with his life. Unlike many budding serial killers, he stayed out of trouble and was a devoted, if somewhat controlling, husband.

However, there were forces at work in Steven Pennell's mind, forces that drove him to assemble a "rape kit" containing pliers, a whip, needles, knives, handcuffs, and other types of restraints. He then started cruising Interstate 40 and Interstate 13, searching for women he could play out his perverted fantasies on. Like so many serial killers before him, he found the perfect victims among the local prostitute population.

Pennell would pick up a victim from a red-light area, drive her to an isolated spot then overpower and bind her. He'd then subject the unfortunate woman to such horrendous torture that death, when it came, must have been a relief. His victims were whipped, bludgeoned with a hammer, tormented with pliers, mutilated with various blades. One had her nipples sliced off while still alive.

Having sated his sick desires, Pennell would then strangle the woman and discard the body along the freeway corridor that gave him his nickname.

Five young women; Kathleen Meyer, 26; Michelle Gordon, 22; Catherine DiMauro; Shirley Ellis; and an unnamed fifth, were sent to their graves before Pennell was eventually caught by an undercover female officer, posing as a prostitute.

Arrested on November 29, 1988, Pennell denied any involvement in the murders. However, after being found guilty of causing two of the five deaths attributed to him, Pennell expressed the desire to be executed. He wanted to spare his family further anguish, he said.

The state of Delaware was happy to grant Pennell his wish. He was sentenced to die by lethal injection in October 1991. He waived all appeals and, despite his wife's vigorous efforts on his behalf, went to the death chamber on March 14, 1992.

Pennel was 34 years old at the time of his execution and was the first man put to death by the state of Delaware in over 45 years.

Thomas Piper

Mention Boston when discussing serial murder and the fiend that springs immediately to mind is the Boston Strangler. But, almost a century before the Strangler terrorized the Massachusetts capital in the 1960's, another depraved killer stalked its streets, his crimes made all the more horrendous because his victims were little girls.

Thomas W. Piper was his name and he was the well-respected sexton of the Warren Avenue Baptist Church. Yet that respectability served only to mask a depraved psychopath with a taste for necrophilia and child rape.

The first murder attributed to the so-called "Boston Belfry Murderer" occurred on the night of December 5, 1873. On that chilly evening, Piper concealed himself in bushes beside a road, then pounced from cover to attack young Bridget Landregan as she passed. Bridget was bludgeoned to death, but before her assailant could rape her body as he had intended, he was scared off by a passing couple. They would later describe the killer as "dark and bat-like," wearing a black opera cloak.

Frustrated by his failure to complete the sexual assault, Piper attacked another woman that same night. This time, he bludgeoned the victim into unconsciousness before raping her. She survived the attack and was able to provide a description her assailant. Once again the black cloak was mentioned and although it got the police no closer to making an arrest, it did tell them that a serial offender was on the loose.

Over the next two years, Piper would remain at large and claim three more victims. In 1874, he clubbed another young girl, Mary Sullivan, to death. Mary Tynan was bludgeoned in her bed in 1875. Although she survived for a year after the brutal attack, she was unable to identify her assailant.

The attacks caused panic and hysteria, with outraged citizens demanding action from the police. They, in turn, threw all of their resources behind the hunt for the killer, but to no avail. Eventually, the police were reduced to taking long shots, like stopping and questioning every man wearing an opera cloak (a move that resulted in these garments going out of fashion while the murderer was at large).

Thomas Piper, of course, was known to wear just such a cloak, but no one suspected the friendly, respectable church sexton of being the killer. It was only once Piper moved away from his regular M.O. that he was eventually caught.

Mabel Hood Young was the five-year-old daughter of a parishioner at Warren Avenue Baptist. On the day of her death, May 23, 1875, Mabel had attended Sunday school with her aunt, but after the class, she had disappeared. The little girl was later found in the church belfry, bludgeoned savagely about the head, and raped. She died of her injuries the next day.

Piper had been seen with Mabel shortly before her disappearance and had been spotted leading her to the belfry. In short order he found himself in custody, being given the third degree by a couple of burly Boston detectives. It wasn't long before he broke down and confessed to killing Mabel, adding that he'd committed three other murders as well, and several rapes.

Piper was tried, found guilty and sentenced to hang. Immediately after sentencing, he retracted his confession. He continued to proclaim his innocence until the day of his execution, when he eventually broke down and admitted his guilt.

Paul Dennis Reid Jr.

Several definitions exist to describe a serial killer. By some of those, Paul Dennis Reid would not qualify. He'd be called a spree killer, such was the explosion of violence he unleashed over just three months in 1997.

His motive, too, is unusual. Some would call it revenge, yet the victims of his murder spree had done him no wrong, were in fact, complete strangers to him. Others would say it was robbery, but the amount of overkill was way beyond what was needed to carry out the heists. Certainly, none of his victims offered resistance. In the end, it might just be that Paul Reid, like others of his ilk, enjoyed the act of murder.

The facts of the case are as follows. On February 15, 1997, Reid was fired from his job as a dishwasher at Shoney's Restaurant in

Donelson, Tennessee, after he threw a plate at a fellow employee in a fit of rage. Reid, a native of Fort Worth, Texas, had recently been released from a 20-year-term for aggravated armed robbery of a Houston steakhouse. He'd come to Nashville hoping to pursue a career as a country music singer.

Still seething over his dismissal, Reid showed up the following morning at Captain D's in Donelson. The store was not yet open, but he managed to talk himself in by pretending he was applying for a job. Once inside, he drew a gun and forced employee Sarah Jackson, 16, and manager, Steve Hampton, 25, into the restaurant's cooler. There he bound their hands and feet before shooting them in the head. He then cleared out the cash registers and fled the scene.

Reid next appeared at a McDonald's outlet in Hermitage, Tennessee, on the evening of March 23, 1997. This time, he waited until the restaurant closed, then forced two employees, Andrea Brown, 17, and Ronald Santiago, 27, back inside as they were leaving.

Finding Robert Sewell, Jr., 23, and José Gonzalez inside, Reid directed all four employees to a storeroom, where he shot and killed Brown, Santiago, and Sewell. However, when he tried to shoot Gonzalez, the weapon jammed. Reid then picked up a knife and stabbed Gonzalez 17 times, leaving him for dead as he fled the store with $3,000 in cash. Gonzalez survived the attack and his later testimony would help convict Reid.

Exactly one month later, on the evening of April 23, 1997, Reid held up a Baskin-Robbins in Clarksville, Tennessee. Following his now familiar M.O. he went to the door after closing and somehow talked the employees into letting him inside. In a variation of what had happened in the previous holdups, he then forced 21-year-old Angela Holmes and 16-year-old Michelle Mace into his car and drove them to Dunbar Cave State Park. Their bodies were found the next day. Both of their throats had been cut.

On June 25, 1997, Reid showed up at the home of the Shoney's manager who had fired him from his dishwashing job. Armed with a knife, he attempted to cut through a screen door. Unable to do so, he eventually left, unaware that the manager's son had filmed the attempted break-in on a camcorder. This was passed on to the police and Reid was arrested soon after.

Given his previous conviction for the steakhouse hold-up in Houston, he immediately came under suspicion as the "Fast Food Killer." Then, after José Gonzalez pulled him from a photo line-up, Reid was formally charged with the murders.

Paul Dennis Reid was convicted on seven counts of first-degree murder across three trials. He received seven death sentences for his convictions, the most ever handed down to a single person in the state of Tennessee. He currently awaits execution at Morgan County Correctional Complex.

Robert Shulman

Robert Shulman has a lot in common with his fellow New Yorker, Joel Rifkin. Like Rifkin, he was a nerdy loser with a taste for drugs and hookers, like Rifkin he was a serial slayer and mutilator of prostitutes. Yet, while "New York Ripper" Rifkin achieved a degree of notoriety (albeit, not of Son of Sam proportions) Shulman is unknown to most. It is difficult to understand why. His crimes were as depraved and brutal as anything witnessed in the Big Apple.

At around 8 a.m. on December 7, 1994, a Suffolk County Public Works employee, driving near the town of Medford, New York, spotted a brand new garbage can lying beside the road. He decided to pick it up but was put off by the smell. On arrival at the depot, he told his supervisor about the incident, mentioning that it smelled as though someone had "dumped a bad load of meat." The supervisor then decided to check it out for himself and drove to where the receptacle lay. The smell was quite horrendous and he soon discovered why. Inside were the dismembered remains of a woman.

On April 6, 1995, employees at a Brooklyn recycling plant discovered a second corpse, this one headless and with its legs severed. The badly battered head was discovered nearby, stuffed into a black plastic bag. Dental records would later identify the victim as Lisa Ann Warner, a known prostitute.

On December 11, 1995, a man searching through the contents of a dumpster for a lost lottery ticket, found what appeared to be a brand new sleeping bag, with something stuffed into it. Coaxing the bag's zipper open, the man got the shock of his life when a human foot protruded. The misplaced lottery ticket forgotten, he ran immediately to call the police.

The victim was a white female with both hands severed at the wrist. She was nude and had suffered severe head trauma. Her left breast bore a tattoo with the name "Melani."

This detail, as well as a physical description of the victim, was released to the media and soon produced an anonymous tip that took investigators to Hollis, Queens. There they interviewed a number of prostitutes and learned that "Melani," was Kelly Sue Bunting, last seen getting into an older model blue Cadillac driven by a white male, a regular along Jamaica Avenue.

Several women who'd been with this man, said that he took them to a home in Nassau County. Later, two of the hookers drove with police to a house in Hicksville, where a 1983 blue Cadillac was parked in the driveway. A check on the license plate revealed that it belonged to a postal worker named Barry Shulman.

Detectives next followed up on the sleeping bag, which was of a brand carried only by Sears. Barry Shulman did not have a Sears account, but his brother Robert did, and had recently purchased the item in question.

On January 4, 1996, investigators placed the Hicksville residence under surveillance. Over the next three months, Robert Shulman was observed driving his brother's car to Queens to solicit prostitutes.

Meanwhile, police firmed up their case against him. Several Jamaica Avenue prostitutes picked him from a photo array as the man last seen with Melani; work schedules proved that he was off duty at the times of the murders and the disposal of the bodies; fibers lifted from his place of work were matched to the victims.

Eventually, on April 6, officers moved in to arrest Shulman. He denied knowing any of the victims but made several incriminating statements under interrogation. A subsequent search of his home produced overwhelming forensic and DNA evidence of Shulman's guilt, including copious amounts of blood spattered over his bedroom walls.

Faced with the overwhelming evidence against him, Shulman broke down and confessed to killing five prostitutes between 1991 and 1996. Speaking in a whimpering voice, he said that he'd taken the women back to his house, plied them with drugs and then bludgeoned them to death with a hammer, a baseball bat or a set of barbells. He'd then dismembered the bodies in his bedroom before disposing of them in landfills and dumpsters.

Shulman was convicted and sentenced to death, his sentence later reduced to life in prison. He died of natural causes on April 13, 2006.

Robert Silveria Jr.

Robert Silveria Jr. is one of the more unusual serial killers you are likely to read about. Known as "Sidetrack," Silveria was a homeless bum, riding the rails and preying on his fellow travelers in order to steal their meager possessions. He would eventually confess to 14 murders and be convicted of two, pulling a life sentence for each. However, detectives who worked the case believe he is responsible for as many as 34 unsolved railroad homicides.

According to Silveria, a gaunt heroin addict with the word "FREEDOM" tattooed across his throat, he was not acting alone. He was a member of the "Freight Train Riders of America," a sort of "hobo mafia." The gang, he said, sprung from a group of disgruntled Vietnam vets, reduced to riding the rails by their desperate circumstances. It is peopled by men with monikers like, Dogman Tony, Desert Rat, Arkansas Bobcat, and Bum Blaster, men who commit murder in order to collect debts and address perceived injustices. Fanciful though this sounds, many law enforcement officers believe that the FTRA is real and that its activities extend to drug trafficking and social security fraud. They also believe that the gang may be responsible for a significant portion of the almost 300 unsolved railroad homicides.

Needless to say, these murders attract very little media attention and almost no investigative effort from the police. But, in the early 1980's, the Los Angeles County Sheriff's Department was alerted to the presence of a possible serial killer riding the rails. The killer's victims were typically shot in the head with a small caliber pistol as they slept in hobo encampments, known as jungles. It was obvious that the unknown killer was a homeless rail rider because he'd have to know the layouts of the camps and also to get in and out unnoticed. Some speculated that he was a "mercy killer," putting bums out of the misery of their shiftless lives. Others believed that he was simply a thrill killer, preying on victims whose deaths would attract little attention.

Faced with the near-impossible task of hunting down a killer amongst the highly mobile and largely uncooperative hobo population, LASD officers set up surveillance on several of the camps. Eventually, after the July 1995 murder of a man named James McLean, their attention fell on Robert Silveria.

A glimpse into Silveria's past offered a hint of the killer that he would become. The product of a violent upbringing, he manifested drug, alcohol, and mental health problems at an early age. When he sought help, he was turned away, an attendant at a clinic once telling him to "take a number, everyone has problems." Silveria would later say that he summoned the image of that indifferent receptionist while he was killing his victims.

Silveria was arrested by a railroad police officer on March 2, 1996, in Klamath Falls, Oregon. He surrendered without a fight, placidly handing over the pistol he was carrying.

Under interrogation, he readily admitted to killing McLean and 13 others in a five-year murder spree that took in Oregon, Utah, California, Arizona, Kansas, and Washington. One of his victims was a college student named Michael Garfinkle, riding the rails for a weekend thrill when he encountered Sidetrack at a switching yard outside Emeryville, California. But all of the others were homeless bums like himself, shot, stabbed or bludgeoned to death for their meager possessions.

Robert Silveria was eventually convicted on two counts of first-degree murder. He is currently serving two consecutive life terms without the possibility of parole, in Oregon.

Morris Solomon Jr.

In November 1998, the world's media was awash with the sensational story of an elderly female serial killer who'd murdered seven of her boarders and buried their bodies in her garden in a downtown Sacramento neighborhood. While stunned readers and viewers contemplated the amazing story of Dorothea Puente, the capture of another Sacramento serial killer, slayer of seven women, caused barely a ripple.

Morris Solomon Jr. was born on March 15, 1944, in Albany, Georgia. Raised by an abusive grandmother who routinely beat him and his brother with switches and electrical cables, he did not meet his parents until be was reunited with them at the age of 13.

The family had since moved to Isleton, a farming town 40 miles from Sacramento. But if Solomon thought this would put an end to his suffering, he was wrong. His parents soon picked up the cudgel, laying into him (and to each other) at the slightest beckoning. His mother also took to verbally abusing the boy in public, and he endured constant ridicule due to her reputation as a "loose woman."

After finishing high school, Solomon tried community college but flunked out and drifted into various jobs, as a carpenter, a mechanic, and a bus driver. He served a year in Vietnam, ending in 1967. After being discharged, he moved to San Francisco, where he married and fathered a child. However, the marriage ended in divorce and he returned to Sacramento.

Shortly after, he acquired his first conviction for sexual assault. Paroled from that term, he returned again to his adopted hometown, where he found work as an itinerant handyman. Soon, though, he would branch out into a deadly sideline in sexual homicide.

Solomon's first known victim was a 22-year-old prostitute named Yolanda Johnson, found inside a closet at one of his previous residences, on June 18, 1986. A month later, Angela Polidore, 25, was found dead, her body concealed under rubble at a site where Solomon had worked as a handyman. Solomon was a suspect in both cases but without sufficient evidence to hold him, the police were forced to let him walk free.

On March 19, 1987, the body of teenage prostitute, Marie Apodoca, was found buried in the yard of an Oak Park, Sacramento, home. Once again, there was a connection to Solomon. He'd lived at the residence until November 1986, which dovetailed nicely with the estimated time of death. However, yet again the police were short on solid evidence. In fact, the state of decomposition was so advanced that it was difficult to prove cause of death.

The circumstantial evidence, though, was piling up. It seemed that a new body turned up wherever Solomon lived or worked. The next to be discovered was 26-year-old Cherie Washington, found in a shallow grave in Oak Park. Then, after two more murder victims – Linda Vitela and Sheila Jacox – were found buried at Solomon's current residence, he was eventually taken into custody. A seventh victim, 29-year-old Sharon Massey, would later be discovered just feet from where Marie Apodoca had been buried.

Charged with seven murders, Solomon when on trial in August 1991 and on the 29th of that month was convicted on all counts. He was sentenced to die by lethal injection, that sentence eventually affirmed by the California Supreme Court on July 15, 2010. He currently awaits execution on death row at San Quentin, California.

Timothy Spencer

In September 1984, police were called to a house in a quiet suburb of Arlington, Virginia. The homeowner, Carolyn Hamm, had been discovered brutally slain. Her nude body lay face down in the garage, her hands bound with a cord from the Venetian blinds. She'd been raped and strangled.

The victim was a respected local lawyer and the area was considered safe and relatively crime free, so the murder caused quite a stir. Pressure was placed on the police to catch the killer and they responded within days. A man named David Vasquez was arrested, tried and convicted for the crime, drawing a 35-year sentence.

Three years later, on December 1, 1987, another murder occurred in the same neighborhood, so similar to the Hamm slaying that police at first thought that a copycat killer was responsible. Forty-four-year-old Susan Tucker was found dead, her nude corpse partially concealed under a sleeping bag. Like Hamms, she'd been bound with cord from the Venetian blinds and the same type of cord had been used to strangle her. She'd also been raped and her killer had apparently masturbated over her corpse, leaving semen stains at the scene.

The murder deeply troubled Detective Joe Horgas. He didn't buy his colleagues theory about a copycat and was convinced that the same man had killed both Hamm and Tucker. That being the case, what had the killer been doing in the intervening three years?

Horgas began making calls to neighboring jurisdictions and soon turned up three similar homicides in Richmond, over 100 miles away. However, all three murders had occurred in the last four months, not spread over the three years, as Horgas had expected.

In September 1987, 35-year-old Debbie Davis had been found raped and strangled to death in her first-floor apartment. Her hands were tied and she'd been killed with a makeshift tourniquet constructed from a sock and a length of pipe. Copious semen stains were left at the scene.

Two weeks later and less than half a mile away, Dr. Susan Hellams was found dead in her bedroom closet. Her hands were tied behind her back and she'd been strangled with a belt. As in the previous cases, the killer had masturbated over the corpse, leaving behind semen stains.

The third victim was 15-year-old Diane Cho, raped and strangled to death in her own bed while her family slept just down the hall. Evidence, in the form of semen stains, was again left at the scene.

Horgas was convinced that all five murders were the work of the same killer, but his theory was roundly rejected by his superiors, citing the timing and physical distance between the crime scenes. Still, Horgas persisted, turning up a series of home invasion rapes that he also believed might be linked.

In January 1988, Arlington PD caught a break with the arrest of a small-time burglar named Timothy Wilson Spencer. Although not initially a murder suspect, Spencer made a number of incriminating statements under interrogation. Further investigation put him in the frame for all five murders and also explained the three-year hiatus and the change of location. Spencer had been in prison during the break in the murders and had been living in a halfway house in Richmond when the murders had occurred there. As an experienced burglar, he also possessed the skills required to break into the victim's homes.

It made a compelling case, but it was not enough to convict Spencer of murder. It would take the fledgling DNA technology to link Spencer to each of the victims and eventually put him on death row.

Timothy Spencer was executed in Virginia's electric chair on April 27, 1994. He entered the history books as the first American convicted of murder on the basis of DNA evidence.

David Vasquez was exonerated of the Carolyn Hamm murder and released, having served five years for a crime he didn't commit.

Paul Michael Stephani

As long as there have been serial killers, there have been serial killers who enjoy taunting the police. From the letters attributed to Jack the Ripper, the mocking phone calls of the Zodiac, to the bizarre scrawlings of the Son of Sam, certain killers just seem to derive some perverse pleasure from taunting their pursuers. Another of this ilk was Paul Michael Stephani, known as the "Weepy-Voice Killer."

On December 31, 1980, Karen Potack had just left a New Year's Eve party in Minneapolis, Minnesota, when she was attacked and savagely beaten with a tire iron. Karen may well have died had it not been for an anonymous call to the police at 3 a.m. that morning. The caller directed police to the site of the attack, near some railroad tracks. "There is a girl hurt there," he said, his voice choked with emotion.

Six months later, on June 3, 1981, Kimberly Compton, 18, was stabbed to death with an ice pick, her killer inflicting 61 wounds in a frenzied attack. Again, police received a call. "Goddamn it, will you find me?" the man said. "I just stabbed somebody with an ice pick. I can't stop myself. I keep killing somebody." He called again two days later, this time apologizing for the murder and promising to turn himself in. He didn't.

The next murder was not initially linked to the series, both because the M.O. was so different, and because the killer didn't call to claim responsibility. Kathleen Greening, 33, was drowned in her bathtub on July 21, 1982. The murder would remain unsolved for 15 years.

Just weeks later, 40-year-old Barbara Simons was stabbed over 100 times in her Minneapolis home. A short while later, the police got another call from the killer. "Please don't talk, listen," he said. "I'm sorry I killed that girl. I stabbed her 40 times."

Other than the phone calls made by the killer, the police had very little to go on. However, they felt that the man had such a unique voice that someone must recognize it. They therefore released several of the tapes to the media in the hope of generating some leads. Over 150 people responded, but the suspects they named were all cleared.

Then, on August 21, 1982, the police finally had a break in the case. A 21-year-old woman named Denise Williams was offered a ride by a stranger. She accepted, but after driving only a short distance the man pulled onto a darkened side street and began attacking her with a screwdriver. Despite being stabbed several times, Williams fought back, striking her assailant on the head with a soft drink bottle. She then managed to get out of the car and escape.

Later that evening, a man walked into the emergency room of a local hospital seeking attention for cuts to his head. By this time, Williams had reported the attack, and the police had warned hospitals to be alert for a man seeking treatment for just such an injury. While Stephani was having his head stitched up, police officers arrived to arrest him for the attack on Williams. Subsequent investigation linked him to the murder of Barbara Simons and he was eventually tried and convicted of both crimes.

Fast-forward to December 1997, and Stephani had served 15 years of a 40-year sentence when he was diagnosed with inoperable cancer. Given less than a year to live, Stephani called for a meeting with Minneapolis homicide investigators.

In a taped confession, he admitted to the murders of Kathy Greening and Kimberly Compton. He also confessed to the New Year's Eve attack on Karen Potack.

Maury Travis

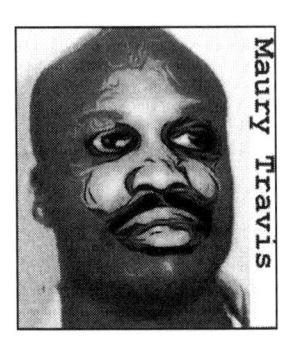

Although the police in St. Louis, Missouri, were reluctant to admit it, a serial killer was preying on the city's prostitute population. The first body, that of 34-year-old Alysa Greenwade, had turned up on April 1, 2001, in Washington Park. She'd been strangled and there were clear signs of sexual torture. Three days later, a woman was found in East St. Louis, severely beaten and close to death. She survived but was unable to identify her attacker. Then, on May 15, the body of Teresa Wilson, 36, was found in West Alton. From her injuries, it seemed that the same man might be responsible, but the police continued to play their cards close to their chest. The killer would slip up sooner or later. They didn't want to cause a panic.

Throughout the rest of the year, the bodies continued to show up with alarming regularity: Betty James, 46, found on May 23; Verona Thompson, 36, found in West Alton on June 29; Yvonne

Crues, 50, discovered on August 25; Brenda Beasley, 33, found in East St. Louis on October 8.

Neither did the new year bring any respite. On January 30, 2002, an unidentified female skeleton was found near Mascoutah. Two more sets of skeletal remains turned up in March bringing the body count to ten. And yet the police had not a single clue they could tie to a suspect.

On May 21, a letter arrived at the offices of the St. Louis Post-Dispatch. Inside were a typed letter and a map indicating the location of yet another body. The letter was passed on to police. Following the directions, they found another unidentified skeleton in West Alton, exactly where the map indicated it would be.

The dumpsite, like the others, carried very little in the way of physical evidence. The map, though, was an entirely different matter. Detectives soon found out that it had been downloaded from the Internet site, Expedia.com. Investigators contacted the company and learned that the information for the map site came from Microsoft. St. Louis PD then called in the assistance of the FBI, who issued Microsoft with a subpoena. What they wanted to know was whether anyone had requested a map of the West Alton area between May 18 and May 21, the dates either side of the postmark on the letter.

Four days later, they had an answer – of sorts. Microsoft was not able to provide a name, but they were able to provide a unique IP address. Next, the Feds contacted WorldCom Inc., the company that provides local telephone numbers to connect Internet services to their dial-up customers. WorldCom had an answer within a day. The temporary IP address had been provided on May 20 to user MSN/maurytravis, who Microsoft later identified as Maury Troy Travis of Ferguson, Missouri.

Armed with this information, St. Louis PD immediately set up surveillance on Travis while they worked on obtaining a search warrant for his home. They learned that Travis was a 36-year-old waiter who had served time for robbery and for various drugs offenses.

Eventually, on June 7, they moved in to arrest Travis, simultaneously serving the search warrant. The search turned up a wealth of evidence including blood splatters found throughout the home, bloodstained belts and ligatures, and various torture paraphernalia. Most damning of all was a collection of videotapes found secreted inside a wall. The tapes showed Travis engaged in bondage and sadistic sex with several women, at least two of whom he appears to murder on film.

DNA evidence has subsequently linked Travis to ten murders. But of the victims whose bodies were found, only one, Betty James, is shown on the tapes. Which begs the question, just how many women did Maury Travis murder?

We shall never know. On June 17, Travis hanged himself in his cell. He had earlier told investigators that he would never go back to prison.

Nathaniel White

On March 22, 1991, the naked body of heavily pregnant mother of two, Juliana Frank, was found dumped near railroad tracks in Middletown, New York. Her killer, Nathaniel White, was well known to police. In fact, he'd just been sentenced to a ludicrously lenient term for the abduction of a 16-year-old girl, although he hadn't begun serving that prison term yet. Still, the police had no reason to connect White to the Juliana Frank murder. A few days later, he handed himself over to begin serving his time. With time off for good behavior, he was released in April 1992.

Following his parole, White returned to Orange County, New York, where he took up with his girlfriend, Jill Garrison. On June 29, Garrison's 14-year-old niece, Christine Klebbe, disappeared. Her family reported her missing on July 1, but it would be a month before her body was discovered near Goshen, New York.

White's next victim was Laurette Reivere, 34, found stabbed and strangled to death in her Middletown home on July 10, 1992. Laurette was the mother of three young children and had worked at Empire Blue Cross/Blue Shield in Middletown.

White next struck on July 20, in Poughkeepsie, New York. Cousins Angelina Hopkins and Brenda Whiteside were last seen leaving the Blue Note Bar in Poughkeepsie with a man driving a pickup truck. Their brutalized bodies would be found August 4 (along with that of Christine Klebbe) after White led investigators to his dumpsite. Both women had been bludgeoned to death, their faces and heads showing evidence of severe blunt force trauma.

The sixth and final victim was Adriane Hunter, 27, found stabbed to death in the early hours of July 30. Adriane had worked with troubled adolescents at Blueberry Treatment Center.

With the murder of Adriane Hunter, the local authorities eventually called in the New York State Police and they began investigating on July 30. By this time, a couple of determined amateur sleuths were already on the case. Angelina Hopkins' mother and sister were unhappy with the lack of attention given to the case by the Poughkeepsie PD. Angelina's sister, Cecelia, had seen her and Brenda Whiteside leave the Blue Note on the night of their disappearance. Now, she and her mother began frequenting the less-than-salubrious tavern, hoping to spot the man they'd left with.

On August 2, White returned to the Blue Note and Cecilia Hopkins learned his name and jotted down his license plate number. She passed this information on to the police and once they learned of White's criminal past, he was pulled in for questioning.

White quickly confessed to the murders and agreed to show police where he'd dumped the bodies. As the convoy drove towards Goshen, he insisted on stopping for pizza. He was chomping on a slice as he pointed out the decomposed remains of the three young women.

White was charged with six counts of murder and entered a plea of not guilty by reason of insanity. His plea cut little ice with the jury who convicted him of all counts on April 14, 1993. He was sentenced to a term of 150 years to life and is currently incarcerated at Great Meadow Correctional Facility in New York.

Scott Williams

Scott Williams is typical of many serial killers. The Monroe, North Carolina native was a nobody, stuck in a dead-end job with the Department of Transport, living an isolated life, a loner with few friends. To those who knew him, he appeared entirely normal. Yet below the surface a toxic cauldron was bubbling, stirring up violent fantasies that became more and more gruesome over time until he could no longer contain them. When the paths between fantasy and reality converged, Williams acted decisively, killing three victims, brutalizing many more, then offering the ludicrous justification, "I didn't mean to hurt them girls."

The three murders occurred over a nine-year period from 1997 to 2006, hardly prolific by the standards of most serial killers. Yet, what Williams lacked in numbers he made up for with the sheer violence of his crimes.

The first victim was Sharon House Pressley, whose sexually mutilated body was discovered in northern Union County, about 10 miles from Williams' home, in 1997. Williams abducted and tortured another woman in 2000, but the victim was able to escape.

Christina "Christy" Parker was not so lucky. Kidnapped by Williams in 2004, she was subjected to even more extreme mutilations than Sharon Pressley, before her body was dumped in the same general area.

The final victim was Sharon Tucker Stone, captured by Williams in 2004, sexually tortured then shot, beheaded, and dismembered. Her body was eventually found in a field in Chesterfield County, South Carolina, in 2006.

One small mercy is that all of the women were killed by bullet wounds to the head before Williams began cutting. That is not to say that they didn't suffer before they were killed. As his surviving victims testified, Williams got off as much on torture as he did on post-mortem mutilations. He even admitted that he tried to cannibalize one of the victims, but after slicing off a chunk of flesh and starting to barbecue it, he was sickened by the smell of broiling meat.

Williams was eventually arrested on March 9, 2006, his home yielding a treasure trove of incriminating evidence, including firearms that would be linked by ballistics to each of the victims. The police also found various knives, whips, chains and restraints.

In addition, Williams supplied blood, hair, and saliva, which would be linked via DNA analysis to his victims.

Williams went on trial in July 2008. In terms of a plea bargain to avoid the death penalty, he entered an Alford plea. That means that he acknowledged that there was enough evidence to convict him of three counts of first-degree murder and that he was prepared to accept the agreed upon sentence.

In addition, he entered Alford pleas to charges of kidnapping, rape and sexual offenses against two more women in 1995 and 2000. The first woman was released by Williams after he'd assaulted her, while the second escaped. Both appeared at the trial to recount their ordeals.

On July 17, 2008, Scott Williams was sentenced to three consecutive life terms. He will never be released.

Martha Woods

Munchausen's Syndrome by Proxy is a rare and bizarre mental illness that most commonly afflicts women. Individuals suffering from the condition are compelled to seek sympathy or attention by making up illnesses for their loved ones, most often children. But the ailments are not always imaginary. Sometimes they are deliberately inflicted by the Munchausen's sufferer. In some instances, the results are deadly.

One such case involved Martha Woods, a military wife who, over a period of 23 years claimed seven young victims including three of her own children, a nephew, a niece, the child of one of her neighbors, and finally, her adopted son.

This killing spree went undetected for almost a quarter-century because Martha was constantly on the move during that time, traveling with her army corporal husband from one military base to another. It prevented doctors from picking up a pattern, stitching together a sequence of 27 life-threatening respiratory attacks, resulting in seven deaths. The fact that Woods was also a pathological liar (another symptom of Munchausen's Syndrome by Proxy) helped conceal her crimes until a suspicious medical examiner finally blew the whistle on her in Baltimore.

The pattern of the attacks was always the same. Woods would arrive at the local hospital in a frantic state, an unconscious child cradled in her arms. Each time, the infant had been alone with Woods when (according to her) it had suddenly stopped breathing. The child was usually revived, stabilized and then sent home with Woods, who made a flamboyant show of concern. Days or sometimes hours later, she'd be back, the child having suffered another attack. On the second or third such visit, the child would inevitably be dead on arrival at the hospital.

The first six deaths were listed as natural, although doctors would admit in hindsight that the symptoms were consistent with deliberate suffocation. Woods played her part in deflecting attention, inventing elaborate charades about vengeful biological parents and strange cars that drifted past her house in the middle of the night.

In one instance, she claimed that the parents of her adopted son wanted their child back and had shown up on her doorstep issuing threats against her and the baby. She even claimed that they'd threatened to burn down her house and led Army CID investigators to a bedroom where flammable liquid had been splashed against a wall.

The agents suspected that Woods had staged the scene herself but they investigated anyway and found that the child's biological parents lived out of state and had not been anywhere near the Woods residence.

Time eventually ran out for Woods in 1969, after her seven-month-old adopted son, Paul, died in Baltimore. A suspicious medical examiner, Vincent DiMaio, decided to look into Woods' past and found that six other children had died in her care since 1940. "As a rule of thumb," DiMaio later said, "One dead baby could be SIDS, two dead babies is suspicious, and three dead babies is homicide."

Found competent to stand trial, Woods was eventually tried for only one murder. However, in a move that would set a precedent in cases of infanticide, evidence of the other deaths was allowed to be entered as evidence. It established quite clearly that Woods was a serial slayer of young children in her care. She was convicted of first-degree murder and sentenced to life in prison.

For more True Crime books by Robert Keller please visit

http://bit.ly/kellerbooks

Printed in Poland
by Amazon Fulfillment
Poland Sp. z o.o., Wrocław